IT'S YOUR BOAT TOO

A WOMAN'S GUIDE TO GREATER ENJOYMENT ON THE WATER

BY

SUZANNE GIESEMANN

Paradise Cay Publications, Inc.
Arcata, California

Cover design by Rob Johnson, www.johnsondesign.org
Editing and Book design by Linda Morehouse, www.WeBuildBooks.com
Copyediting by Ruth E. Hardy

Interior photographs by Suzanne Giesemann and Ty Giesemann
Cover photo and author photo © by Billy Black, www.BillyBlack.com

Cover image: Morris 42 with author Suzanne Giesemann at the helm.
The Morris 42 won *Cruising World*'s Domestic Boat of the Year 2006.
www.morrisyachts.com

Printed in the United States of America
3rd Printing. 2009
ISBN 978-0-939837-69-2

Published by Paradise Cay Publications, Inc.
P. O. Box 29
Arcata, CA 95518-0029
800-736-4509
707-822-9163 Fax
paracay@humboldt1.com

For my father and mother,
Bill and Ruth Smeltzer,
who taught me how to walk, tie my shoes,
and enjoy boats.

CONTENTS

PART III: UNDER WAY

APPENDICES

OTHER BOOKS BY SUZANNE GIESEMANN

Conquer Your Cravings

Living a Dream

The Priest and the Medium

ACKNOWLEDGMENTS

As always, I give my love and appreciation to my husband and sailing partner, Ty. Having been a Navy destroyer captain and seamanship instructor, he could have written this book. Unfortunately, even though he considers himself "a New Age kind of guy," he wouldn't have done well with the woman-to-woman perspective. Ty, you gave me just what I needed: the right amount of technical advice to keep me out of trouble, and an endless supply of understanding when I was glued to my keyboard for hours on end.

Thanks and a big hug to Dahleen Castleberry—the best student a teacher could ask for, and a great friend. As I wrote this book, Dahleen, I just imagined the two of us sitting in the cockpit discussing all this good stuff while Rudy chewed on your shoelaces. Thanks for your encouraging words and your willingness to try anything. May all women boaters share your boundless enthusiasm.

Finally, I feel blessed to have found not only an outstanding editor, but a new friend in Linda Morehouse. Linda, you took what could have been a tedious process and made it thoroughly enjoyable. Thanks for your superb suggestions, your professionalism, patience, and consistently good humor. When you're ready for a break from all your hard work, let's go sailing!

Foreword

Serenity was the only word to describe the morning: sparkling sunshine, charming vistas, Larry rowing easily and steadily across the estuary. Astern lay *Seraffyn*, the fine little sailing vessel that had carried us from California, south along the coast of Mexico and Central America, then eastward into the Caribbean and onward across the Atlantic. Ahead lay the centuries-old buildings of Falmouth, our favorite port in England and the one I'd chosen as my base while Larry went off to race around Britain and Ireland on another man's yacht.

Just before we reached the landing closest to the bus station, Larry shattered my peace of mind by saying, "I hope you take *Seraffyn* out for a bit of sailing while I'm away. Remember, she's your boat too." In the hustle of off-loading his sea bag and saying farewell I didn't get around to answering him.

Larry had been a professional sailor when I met him, with several thousand sailing miles under his belt; I had been a complete neophyte. Everything I knew about sailing I had learned under his tutelage over the previous eight years. We'd been cruising offshore for five of those years and I'd often taken the helm, been in full charge while he slept, and tried my hand at each and every aspect of sailing the boat—but always with Larry taking the lead or at least being near at hand to offer advice or bail me out if things went wrong. I'd heard him tell other folks (usually men and usually when I was within earshot) of his complete trust in my ability to take charge if something happened to him.

As I rowed away from Falmouth back toward *Seraffyn* that June morning in 1974 I tried to ignore the challenge he'd thrown to me. I had lots to fill the next six or eight weeks: the local village water festival I'd offered to help with, the International 14 championship race committee duties I'd volunteered for at the local yacht club, writing projects, and a trip to London to meet up with my parents. I'd never once thought of going sailing just to go sailing. In fact I began to wonder if I really liked sailing or liked living with Larry, for whom sailing was almost as important as eating.

As I climbed back on board *Seraffyn* and began securing the dinghy painter, a young couple who spent their summers on the boat moored just astern rowed by to invite me over for morning tea. I couldn't believe the words that came out of my mouth: "Grab your scones and a jacket. Let's take *Seraffyn* out for a spin."

I'll never forget the exquisite joys of that first time I truly realized *Seraffyn* was my boat too—mine to command, mine to point in any direction I felt like taking her, mine to damage if I was careless. Over the next weeks I took her a good distance, usually with friends I invited to join me, sometimes completely on my own.

I had some grand mini-adventures on this lovely engineless 24' cutter. But one of the best of all was sailing in to Plymouths' Mill Bay Docks 40 miles from Falmouth the day before the start of Larry's race, and, in answer to his question of how I got there, saying, "Sailed here." My chest swelled as I heard him tell other racers, "Lin's great to sail with; she can handle *Seraffyn* as well as I can." Though I felt he was exaggerating, I had learned many new things about myself and about sailing. But even more important, by finally deciding it was my boat too and going out without Larry's guiding hand on board, I'd had fun, real fun, the kind adults—and especially women—rarely have. There is an amazing joy in being in control, in playing with something as large and powerful as a sailing or cruising powerboat, in learning new tricks and skills, even in making mistakes (preferably out of sight of others, as I did while practicing a few of the maneuvers I planned to use when I got into harbors), then finding ways to avoid them. Suzanne Giesemann has felt it; you can tell from her writing and the stories she uses to illustrate this book.

There is something else I gained from those days when I alone chose whether or not I felt like going sailing. I learned the pressures there are on the person in charge, especially if his crew does not have the knowledge, skills, or interest necessary to assist in the maneuvers of getting under way or keeping watch or docking. Communicating clearly with the guests I brought along, being in charge of making sure lines were properly laid out, properly secured, showed me clearly lessons Larry had tried to teach, often to the point of sounding like a nag.

From that experience and others that followed, Larry and I developed a rule we have used during the 180,000 miles and 40 years we have sailed together: it is our job to make each other look good. Or put more crudely: cover the other guy's rear end. Because of my knowledge of boat handling and seamanship, plus what he puts down to woman's intuition, Larry feels I have spotted many potential problems before they caused more than a slight change in plans: from simple things like spotting chafe on a line, or a potential navigation error, to spotting more serious problems, such as noting the change in engine tone during a delivery trip that signaled a developing fuel pump problem.

Though you may never feel the desire to set off for a day or a week without your partner, *It's Your Boat Too* is an amazingly readable guide to the knowledge that will let you be a true participant afloat.

Suzanne says by learning more about your boat you will have more fun. The knowledge she shares here could even save your life or your partner's life in that one-in-a-thousand situation.

Just as important, but more probable, by getting more involved and understanding ways to make your partner look good as you come into a marina or get under way, you could turn boating into a pleasurable pastime that, instead of threatening the core of your relationship, strengthens your respect for each other and helps you build a warm working partnership both afloat and ashore.

—Lin Pardey, Kawau Island, New Zealand, 2006

INTRODUCTION

I am addicted.

I'm addicted to boats.

I love being on them and around them. So I went to a few boat shows recently, where I gave a series of seminars on Women in Boating. It was an enlightening experience. Not the seminars, so much as the human interaction before and after the presentations.

That's when I heard all the fascinating comments.

I'm not talking about remarks from the Neanderthal men. You know—the ones in ball caps and t-shirts who stuck their head in the seminar room while I was setting up and asked, "So where are all the chicks?"

Nor am I talking about the joker who asked, "Why do you want women to take the wheel of a boat when they can't even drive a car?"

Those guys I just ignored.

No, I'm talking about comments from ordinary men and women that gave me insight into a problem I've long suspected exists: There are a lot of women out there who don't enjoy this whole boating thing nearly as much as their partners do.

I'd ask women passing by my booth if they were going to attend my Women in Boating seminar. All too frequently a good prospect would shrink away from me, point at her partner, and say, "Oh, no.

That's *his* thing. I'm just here to keep him company."

"Isn't it your boat, too?" I'd ask. To which she'd invariably respond, "Well, yeah, but I just handle the lines."

Her partner would stand there like a little boy, his face eager but sheepish.

"You should go, honey," he'd urge.

But of course, I'd never see her again. And what a shame that was. Those who did attend came away enthused, empowered, and excited about taking on a new and improved role aboard their vessel.

You see, Ratty had it right in Kenneth Grahame's 1908 book, *The Wind in the Willows,* when he said, "There is absolutely nothing half so much worth doing as simply messing about in boats."

There's something magical about boats. Maybe it's how they carry you away from the stress of daily life. Maybe it's the thrill of a speedboat powering through the waves at full throttle, or the serenity of a sailboat silently harnessing the wind. Whatever it is, boats have a special allure.

So my question for you is: *Why should men have all the fun?*

I've been having fun on boats my whole life. Literally. When I was a newborn baby in Pennsylvania's Harrisburg Hospital my dad took our Trojan runabout up the Susquehanna River, stopping just below the maternity ward window so my mom could wave my tiny hand down at him. It wasn't long before I was going along for the ride, swaddled in a pink blanket up under the cuddy cabin.

I drove a boat long before I drove a car. As an adult, I've owned five different sailboats ranging from 35 to 46 feet. I even sailed one across the ocean. I've had plenty of chances to serve as "First Mate," but trust me, I never got the t-shirt. Truthfully, I didn't want it.

Don't misunderstand me. There's nothing wrong with being the Mate. It's a valued and necessary position on any vessel. But I've also been the co-captain, and I'm here to tell you, it's a heck of a lot more fun when you share the load.

Women get pigeonholed into being the Mate. Tradition and culture place us in the secondary role. Unfortunately, many men are happy to let us stay there. But women have been breaking stereotypes for decades. It's no big deal. Believe me, as a woman who served twenty years in the Navy and watched "the weaker sex" go from strictly support functions to captains of warships, I know all about expanding roles and breaking glass ceilings.

I'm also well aware that in a boating emergency there can only be one captain. When things get dicey, one person has to call the shots, and that should be the person with the most experience. In many cases, that will be the man. But in all other circumstances, the little lady shouldn't be relegated to the foredeck or the galley simply because tradition dictates it.

Maybe you're perfectly content to be the Mate. And that's fine. I'm simply asking you to step beyond your self-imposed limits and see what happens. If you're willing to try on a new role, you may just find yourself having more fun on your boat than you ever thought possible. If you don't like being co-captain, at least you'll be a far more skilled and knowledgeable Mate who could take over if need be.

And that's what this book is all about. The basic premise is simple: It's only fun for so long to merely go along for the ride. The more you get involved in boating or sailing, the more you'll enjoy it.

So I want you to commit the following phrase to memory:

There is nothing on a boat a man can do that a woman can't.

Well, actually, I'm wrong. There is one thing. We can't pee over the rail. But considering that doing so can easily lead to a man-overboard situation, I don't recommend it for either sex. All other boating activities, however, are gender-neutral. Driving, docking, navigating, performing maintenance . . . you can do it *all.* You, too, can be an equal partner aboard your vessel.

Okay. Back up a second. I want to know what thought went through your mind when you read that last sentence. Did you embrace the idea of being as knowledgeable as the captain, or even becoming a co-captain, as something radical yet possible? Or did you shrink back like some of those women I met at the boat shows?

If the latter, I have my work cut out for me. In either case, read on. I've been told my addiction for boats is contagious. If I do this right, some of that wonderful obsession may rub off on you.

In this book I'm going to show you how to get the most out of your time on the water. I'll tell you how to deal with things that can detract from your enjoyment and show you ways to make the whole experience more enjoyable. You'll learn how to deal with any fears you may have. You'll also get an introduction to the basic skills a boater should master to be considered a safe and competent mariner, and you'll understand why it's important to have them.

My goal in this book is to encourage and empower you to the point where you'll get out there and try new things. I want you to ***think beyond the lines.*** Do this and you'll be a safer and more competent mariner. Do this and you'll be tremendously proud of yourself. Do this and you'll have a lot more fun.

Do this because it's your boat, too.

Part I

Women and Boats

1

What's So Great About Boating?

Welcome to the world of boating. I won't lie and say it's nothing but wonderful and idyllic moments. There are those, to be sure. But like everything, there are times on a boat when you wish you'd taken up horticulture instead.

I'm here to tell you that when you set yourself up for success and approach boating with the right attitude, it can be an exciting, rewarding, and challenging sport that offers you as much in return as you put into it. Whether you're new to boating or an old hand, there's always more to learn and more adventures to be had.

Boating is an activity that appeals to thousands, as evidenced by the proliferation of boats at marinas or on trailers around the country. Whether it's along the coasts, or on bays, rivers, or lakes, people everywhere love to get out on the water. Vessels from small skiffs to large, gleaming yachts fit the category of "pleasure boats," as long as pleasure is their main raison d'être. Unfortunately, there are a lot of women out there who can't seem to find the pleasure in the boat.

I could stop now and make a list of the reasons why this is so, but we'll get to that in good time. Trust me. For now, I want to focus on the one reason women fail to maximize their enjoyment of boating that supersedes all others. I raised this point in the introduction, so it won't come as a complete surprise that it's only fun for so long to simply go along for the ride.

That may seem self-evident, but since boating is a sport, let me use a sports analogy to make this point even more apparent.

Picture your average American couple. Let's call the husband Ralph and the wife Sheila, simply because I don't know anybody by those names. Ralph comes home one day and announces, "Guess what, honey? I bought us some golf clubs and signed us up for a membership at Rolling Hills."

Now, golf has never been at the top of Sheila's priority list, and she thinks Rolling Hills sounds like a cemetery, but it's obvious Ralph is excited about this new activity. Sheila likes to see her honey happy, so she decides to give it a try. Ralph spends the rest of the week reading *Golfing for Dummies* and offers her a copy of *Golf Made Simple*, but she's not interested enough to read a book about it. After all, this was his idea. She figures she can learn as she goes.

Saturday rolls around and it's a beautiful day. As Sheila leaves the clubhouse with her new golf bag swung over her shoulder, she looks up at the blue sky and realizes it's pretty nice to get to spend the day outdoors.

Ralph has been practicing his swing all week, so he volunteers to go first. He hits the ball a respectable distance down the fairway and turns to Sheila with a beaming smile. She's up.

Sheila grips the club and swings away. Noticing with surprise that her ball is still sitting on the tee, she suddenly and painfully becomes aware that people are watching. She swings again, but her club hits the ground with a thud, propelling nothing into the air but a divot of dirt. Ralph steps in now, eager to provide some expert instruction. After all, he read the book. Standing behind her, he puts his hands over Sheila's and shows her exactly how to grip and swing the club.

The crowd of onlookers is growing and Sheila is starting to sweat. The third time's a charm, however, as she connects with the ball and sends it dribbling into the weeds fifty feet to her right.

Some fun, huh?

After 18 holes of this misery, Sheila fails to see what's so great about chasing the stupid ball around. Ralph, meanwhile, has had a great time. He's oblivious to Sheila's discomfort and is already talking about next weekend's game.

The following Saturday is another gorgeous day. Sheila doesn't want to ruin it with another bout of public humiliation, so she makes her husband a deal. She'll keep him company on the course, but she doesn't care to play.

"Great," Ralph says, relieved and thrilled that she still wants to share his new interest with him. "You can be the caddy."

Out on the course, Sheila's a great help. She hands Ralph whatever he asks for and even fetches drinks. It's nice to be outside again getting some exercise, but he seems to be having a lot more fun than she is. But this is as involved as Sheila cares to get; the memories from last week still sting. At least she's handling the clubs, walking the greens—that's all part of golf, too, isn't it?

Too many women boaters are like Sheila. They just go along for the ride. Yes, they handle the lines and serve food, but not much else. They enjoy boating because they're outside, on the water, spending time with their husbands away from the house. But many parts of the sport remain a mystery or are too intimidating to practice in public.

After a couple of embarrassing moments when they didn't know how to do something or, worse yet, did something and were told they did it "wrong," they're no longer willing to put any effort into learning or doing more. Their husbands' helpful suggestions are beginning to sound an awful lot like orders. Pain has taken the pleasure out of pleasure boating.

But there must be something about boating that attracts people to it in the first place and keeps so many coming back. If a few bad experiences have soured you on taking a more active role, or if you're still trying to figure out what this boating thing is all about, let's review some of the finer points of the sport.

Why? Well, a good marriage counselor will tell you that if you're having trouble with your husband, you should go back to when you first fell in love and focus on all the things that attracted you to him in the first place. Similarly, if you fail to find the pleasure in boating, a little reminder of its positive aspects may help you fall in love all over again.

First and foremost, boating is fun. Cyndi Lauper told us a long time ago that "girls just wanna have fun." Well girls, if you've ever blasted along in a speedboat, or been on a sailboat that was trimmed just right, you know what I'm talking about. You're out there on the water, away from the grind of your daily life. It's different, it's enjoyable, it's entertaining, all of which are synonymous with that little three-letter word: f-u-n.

My husband, Ty, and I think fun should be shared with others, so we often invite guests aboard our boat. When we take someone who's never been out on a boat before, their reaction is always the same. They're excited and all smiles as we start the engine and take in the dock lines. Then, when we put the engine in gear and pull away from the pier, their smiles change to a look of wonder. Their eyes widen and their mouths gape as they watch the land recede.

They invariably blink and say, “Wow...” as they suddenly comprehend the unique sense of independence known only to boaters. Out there on the water there are no roads restricting you, no speed limits holding you back. You can turn right if you feel like it, left when the mood strikes, or maybe, just maybe, keep going forever . . . .

Okay, I know there are rules to be followed, restricted channels, and no-wake zones to obey. You still have duties and deadlines waiting ashore. But once you're out there, your boat is your island—your own private oasis.

It's hard to deny that there's a certain “something” about boats that causes even landlubbers to look at them longingly. Whether it's a classic schooner with a sharply raked bow or a sleek and shiny speedster, boats make us stop and stare.

I've watched plenty of people walking the docks at marinas. I've seen that far-off look in their eyes as they gaze longingly at all those adult toys, and I know what that look is. It's their brain taking a mental time-out as they shift into dream mode.

You see, boats represent freedom—freedom from the strains of everyday life. We fantasize about getting away from it all, but boats turn those fantasies into reality. Step aboard a boat and you leave your stress behind. No more alarm clocks, traffic, road rage, or rudeness; no work, crowds, errands, or attitude . . . . Like a magic carpet, boats carry you to a better place.

I recently learned that only 20 percent of boaters take their boats out overnight. I was floored that 80 percent of boat owners are strictly day sailors who never go to anchor. While it's true that you can reap the same stress-reducing rewards from just a short day trip, there's nothing like the serenity of spending the night “on the hook.”

Imagine sitting on the deck of your boat, surrounded by water. A sandy beach curves around you a little way off, keeping you snug and sheltered. As your dinner cooks on a rail-mounted grill, you sip on a drink. Perhaps there's some soft jazz playing in the cabin, or maybe your only music is the song of the sea birds off your beam. In either case, before you go below, you pull out your camera to capture that incredible orange and purple sunset. It just never seemed that pretty at home.

Because you've chosen a well-protected spot, you gently rock to sleep with the water quietly lapping at your hull. The next day you climb into the cockpit and breathe in the crisp morning air. That first cup of coffee tastes especially good while you enjoy the silence that clings to you like the drops of dew on the deck.

Congratulations, you're experiencing one of those "It doesn't get any better than this" moments. These are frequent occurrences when you venture out overnight. Try it; you'll be hooked.

Do you like nature? Being on a boat gives you opportunities to get up-close and personal with a wide variety of God's creatures, both large and small, that you'll never see if you stay ashore. We've had 70-foot whales surface next to our 46-foot sailboat. Porpoises regularly play in our bow wave where we can almost reach down and touch them. Spend any time at all on the water and you may need to invest in a bird book to identify the many species that fly by to check you out.

Enjoy travel? A boat can give you as much as you want. As you gain more experience and your skills increase, so can the distance you cover. In smaller boats you can explore neighboring waters. Overnight trips will double your range. If you hunger for more adventure, look into bigger, more seaworthy vessels, or check out chartering. There are boats for hire all over the world.

One of the most popular chartering spots is the British Virgin Islands. Ty and I chartered a boat for the first time in the BVI. We flew into Tortola and signed out a 40-foot sloop. The boat was fresh from the factory. After seven days of idyllic sailing from island to island and sipping Pain Killers[1] in postcard-perfect settings, we realized once again that all this fun was just too good not to share.

So after saving our pennies for a couple of years, we invited my sister and brother-in-law to join us on another sailing vacation. This time we ventured a little farther . . . to the French Riviera. Talk about a great place to charter. It's one thing to explore Provence by car, but it's altogether more exciting to sail your "own" vessel into the harbors of Monaco, Nice, and Cannes. Our 38-footer looked like a dinghy next to some of those megayachts, but we doubt their guests were having any more fun than we were. Of course, the topless women on the beach at St. Tropez may have influenced my brother-in-law's vote, but we all agreed it was the best vacation we'd ever had.

All thanks to a boat.

Chartering is more affordable than many people realize, and it's available to anyone with a desire for travel and adventure. If you lack the skills to set out solo, you can always hire a captain. In either case, whether you're chartering in exotic places or enjoying your familiar home waters, you're bound to experience boat math. Nautical arithmetic says that one boat plus one boat equals at least two cocktails and one potluck supper.

That's because boating is synonymous with camaraderie. There's a timeless tradition that holds that sailors will always help another sailor in need. This translates into an instant bond among boaters. No matter what your background or beliefs, there is an unspoken understanding among those who share the love of the water based on a respect for Mother Nature and the knowledge that they will be there for each other if the need ever arises.

---

[1] BVI Pain Killer: 2 oz. cream of coconut, 2 oz. orange juice, 8 oz. pineapple juice, 4 oz. rum. Blend, shake, or stir without ice. Pour into big glass filled with ice and grate fresh nutmeg on top. Serves two.

After years of cruising aboard our boat, our best memories come not from the places we've visited, but from the friends we've made.

Boating also offers quality time with the family. In today's busy world, competing demands keep Mom, Dad, and the kids constantly running in different directions. But when you get out on the water, you're all, well, in the same boat. The whole family can enjoy swimming, fishing, eating, playing games . . . whatever . . . together.

Some parents take their children long-term cruising with them. Boats with cruising kids have a way of finding others so the children have playmates. These youngsters don't spend hours in front of a computer screen or a TV. They're outdoors most of the day, learning new skills, engaged in challenging activities. Cruising kids are some of the most well-adjusted children we've met.

If boating is so great, why aren't more women involved in it? Because it's traditionally a male-dominated sport. But that's changing. More and more women are discovering how enjoyable it is to get out on the water and take an active role. The more you get involved, the more fun it becomes. This is a basic truth you must embrace if you're going to enjoy boating as much as your partner does.

Yes, boating is challenging. Yes, there's a lot to learn to do it well. Yes, it has its uncomfortable moments. But we'll deal with those issues in due course. Like falling in love all over again, you should focus on the positives, because the secret is out: boating is fun. It's relaxing. It offers independence, freedom, and endless opportunities for travel and adventure. It gives you a chance to interact with nature, reconnect with your family, and make new friends.

Can't say the same about horticulture.

2

ATTITUDE IS EVERYTHING

One of the best quotes I ever saw was on a bumper sticker from the boating magazine *Latitudes and Attitudes*. It read:

Attitude: The difference between ordeal and adventure

I'd been walking past a sailing friend's car, but when I read that phrase, I stopped as if struck. The meaning of those words and their application to what was going on in my life at the time really hit home. Ty and I had recently been discussing the possibility of making a long passage in our sailboat, and I was hesitant to agree to what for me would be a major undertaking.

Suddenly I realized that I'd been looking at the voyage in the wrong light—as an ordeal. Treading carefully, I tested the idea that an offshore passage didn't have to be an ordeal. It could, in fact, be a great adventure. It was all up to me and how I looked at it. Like putting a smile on your face when you're down in the dumps, once I made that shift in my attitude, the effect was immediate. By changing the way I thought about the idea, I was instantly more positive and willing to consider it.

I'm well aware that taking a boat offshore is not something all boaters care to do. That's understandable. But the fact that the way you think about something affects how much you enjoy it is universal. It applies to all boaters—brave or timid, experienced or novice, knowledgeable or naive. If you approach boating with a positive attitude, your enjoyment will automatically increase.

In the first chapter I discussed the things that make boating so pleasurable. High on the list was stress relief. As I wrote those words, I knew there was a chance that some readers might roll their eyes and say, "Relax on a boat? Yeah, right."

I hope that wasn't you.

If stepping aboard your boat only adds to your stress, then you need to figure out what it is about boating that you don't like. Does your partner turn into Captain Bligh when he gets behind the helm? Do you simply follow orders without knowing what to do next? Do you worry because you wouldn't know how to react in an emergency? Are you frightened by the water, the waves, or unknown threats? Have you had a bad experience on the water that made you feel threatened?

Examine what it is about boating that you don't like, then ask yourself how you could improve upon it. Often the best place to start when you want to change something for the better is with your attitude.

Now, I'll be the first person to admit that there are times when being on the water isn't necessarily pleasant. We once bought a 44-foot ketch, a classic-looking vessel that was built to last. I thought it would be our ideal cruising boat. Like most boats, it was a major investment in money and emotion. To get her home, we had to take her out in the Gulf Stream from Florida to Maryland. Within hours of getting under way, we got caught in conditions that the National Weather Service hadn't predicted. Twelve-foot seas and gale-force winds for three interminable days did nothing to help me bond with this new vessel. By the time we pulled into port, I detested everything about that boat. I never wanted to set foot on her again. And in fact, we immediately put the boat on the market.

For me, that whole experience was an ordeal. It left me battered and bruised, both physically and mentally. Besides being a financial disaster, it left me wondering if long-term cruising was really for me.

Luckily, time mends the body and the mind. I'd been on the water enough to know that good far outweighs the bad. When enough time had passed to let me look at the situation rationally, I was able to see the mistakes we'd made.

Only after we found ourselves in an unpredicted gale did we discover how wet, uncomfortable, and unstable the boat was. Its very low freeboard and open helm station allowed waves of green water to wash through the cockpit, threatening to take me with them. The water repeatedly rose above my yellow sea boots, soaking my socks. Below decks I was bashed around, unable to cook or sleep. Leaking ports left everything a soggy mess.

No, there was little about that voyage that qualified as an adventure.

My point in dredging up those bad memories is this: If you want to enjoy boating, you need to set yourself up for success. Make sure you have a boat that you feel safe on and that makes you happy. Know how the boat handles and how to handle her before taking her in conditions that might deteriorate. And don't get caught with a schedule that causes you to go out on the water in spite of poor weather.

If the whole point of pleasure boating is pleasure, do everything you can to make it so.

Granted, boating is an outdoor sport. This means you have to deal with Mother Nature. She's a tough old broad, and you want to give her all the respect she deserves, but that doesn't mean you have to be cold, hot, wet, and miserable. Don't like the sun? Invest in a bimini—a canvas covering to keep the sun off. Always cold on the water? Buy clothing made with the latest outdoor fabrics and learn how to layer. Don't like getting wet when the clouds dump a load of rain on you?

That's what foul-weather gear is for.

The first time Ty and I sailed in the rain together, I put on my foulies and joined him in the cockpit. He looked at me strangely and asked why I didn't go below. I realized that this was one of those cultural issues. You know: Little boys jump in puddles and slosh around; little girls are told to come in out of the rain.

Well, I'm not a little girl anymore. I explained to him that if he was going to be out there, so was I. It was my boat, too.

Please understand, I am like a cat. I hate getting wet. But with rubber boots, a rain hat, and a set of really cool-looking yellow overalls and jacket, I can stand in the pouring rain and smile.

And so can you if you have the right attitude. When the sky opens up, do you scurry to get out of the rain, or do you get out there and splash in the puddles?

Whether you look at boating as an ordeal or as an adventure is completely up to you. The past is in the past. You may have had some unpleasant experiences on the water, but you don't have to repeat them. Use them as learning experiences, because they always are.

If there are still things that you don't like about being out on your boat, ask yourself what you can do to improve them. Sometimes this can be as easy as changing your thoughts. Other times it means buying things for yourself or your boat that will make boating more pleasant and comfortable. It's far easier to have a positive attitude when you're warm, dry, cozy, and relaxed.

Remember, however, that we are talking about the nautical environment here. There will always be a certain potential for discomfort or frustration. The goal is not to let such situations overshadow the potential for pleasure. For that reason, I want to teach you an attitude-saving phrase. You are to repeat this phrase whenever you catch your teeth clenching, your hands balling into fists, or a shriek of frustration welling up in your throat.

Here it is:

It's the nature of boats.

This is a simple phrase, but those five words can turn your attitude around 180 degrees in an instant. They can shift your frustration to amusement, allowing you to shake your head and laugh at the irony of any situation.

Boats are on the water, so there will be times you get wet when you didn't intend to. Tell yourself "it's the nature of boats"; put on some foul-weather gear and a smile. Boating is an outdoor sport, so you may get hot or cold. Repeat your new mantra and put up an awning or add a layer of fleece. Boating requires dealing with ropes (usually called lines), and they often get tangled. It's the nature of lines. Repeat that attitude-saving phrase, and, well, I think you get the idea.

The difference between ordeal and adventure lies within you. It starts with your thoughts—with the way you think about boating.

No matter your skill level, no matter your experience, no matter whether your partner is Captain Bligh or Captain America, you control your thoughts; nobody else does. The weather doesn't ruin your day. Neither does the sea state, your boat, or your mate. Your own thoughts do.

When you change your attitude, you change your experience. The boating adventure is yours for the taking.

3

Your Role On Board

I want you to complete the following sentence with the first thing that comes to mind:

"A woman's role on board is usually ______."

What did you come up with? Perhaps it was "the line handler," or maybe "a galley slave." Men trying to be funny might say, "to look pretty."

Funny or not, these are the most common roles women fill on board pleasure boats. There's nothing wrong with being the line handler. It's an essential job. Anyone who has singlehanded a boat knows the challenge of trying to steer and secure dock lines at the same time. Having a dedicated line handler greatly decreases the chances of damaging your boat.

Being the ship's cook is also important if you're going to be under way for more than a few hours. But "galley slave" indicates that's all the cook does—she spends her time under way stuck in the galley. I know more than a few women who can identify with the title.

I know a woman who used to fill all three of the roles I mentioned quite well. She handled the lines, could whip up some tasty meals in her galley, and looked pretty darned good doing it. Unfortunately for her, that's all she did, and she wasn't happy about it.

I'm talking about my friend Dahleen. Unlike "Sheila" in my golfing analogy, Dahleen is a real person and that's her real name. I try to be clever, but I'm not creative enough to come up with a unique name like that.

Dahleen wears hip-hugging jeans and slimming sweaters like a woman half her age, and believe me, she can get away with it. She's cute and petite, with a personality that sparkles like her dark Latina eyes. Her enthusiasm for life is infectious, so it's no wonder she was excited about *Into the Light*, the 41-foot sloop she and her husband recently bought.

Like many couples who enjoy the water, Dahleen and Greg dreamed of leaving behind the daily grind and sailing off into the sunset. They'd chartered boats in years past and had a great time. The problem was, Greg did most of the sailing while Dahleen sunned herself on the foredeck. This arrangement suited them both at the time, but now Dahleen found herself the co-owner of a boat that would soon become their life's focus.

She realized she was in unfamiliar territory. Greg was serious about cruising, and she wanted to share the dream with him. The problem was, she was far behind her husband in experience. Dahleen told me, "I felt like it was Greg's boat. He did everything and I just pulled in the lines or sat waiting for the next command. I really didn't know what to do."

It's understandable that this passive role was hard for Dahleen to accept. She'd been a take-charge sergeant in the army. She was now a successful businesswoman. It rubbed her the wrong way to have to wait until Greg told her when and how to do things.

Sensing her frustration and her desire to enjoy the new boat as much as her husband, I suggested she enroll in a sailing school for women only. I'd heard lots of good things from women who attended classes where nobody pressured them or yelled. I felt she would benefit from an all-inclusive course that would get her started toward being on par with her husband's skills. Greg was all for the idea and encouraged Dahleen to take a week off work to attend such a school.

A month later Ty and I met Dahleen and Greg for dinner aboard *Into the Light*. Dahleen had taken my advice seriously and showed me a stack of brochures touting various schools. While sipping a glass of wine in the cockpit, I asked if any of the classes looked right for her.

"They all look pretty good," she said, then added coyly, "but I was hoping you'd teach me, instead."

I must admit that her request caught me off guard. True, I had years of sailing experience and I kept my captain's license current. I'd been a part-time instructor at a co-ed school in Seattle and a safety officer on the Naval Academy's 44-foot sloops. But I had never given private lessons and would have to come up with a syllabus from scratch.

Dahleen reminded me that Ty had a business trip coming up. She knew I'd be alone all week, and generously offered my teaching her as a way to fill my time. What a pal.

The more I thought about the idea, the more I liked the prospect of having such an eager student with no bad habits to unlearn. I was impressed with Dahleen's desire and figured if she was serious enough to give up a week's vacation to learn how to sail, I could hardly say no. I agreed to come up with a schedule that would run from Monday through Friday with both classroom and hands-on lessons. There was just one condition. I turned to Greg and smiled as I informed both of them that all sailing and docking practice would have to be aboard their new boat.

To his credit, Greg showed little reaction. Well, ok, he may have cringed just a little, but he kept a smile pasted on his suddenly pale face. How could he argue that the best way for his wife to learn to handle a boat would be to learn on the very boat she'd be cruising?

We sealed the deal over dessert. When Greg and Dahleen went back to their home in Tennessee, I remained in Charleston and came up with a syllabus that covered everything the professional schools did. By the time Dahleen returned, I had a schedule that optimized every minute of the next five days.

There was only one problem: she didn't come alone.

She called me from her cell phone. "I'm here in the parking lot," she said, "but Greg's with me."

As if she could hear my teeth gritting through the phone, she quickly added, "But he just came to share the long drive. He's staying until Wednesday, but you won't even know he's here."

"We can't have him around," I said firmly. "I don't want anything to affect your confidence. This is your time."

Dahleen assured me Greg had plenty of errands to run and would stay out of our way.

Hmmmmm.

When I showed up at their slip at 8 A.M. on Monday, she had the boat familiarization checklist I'd previously sent her open on the salon table and was going over systems. Greg was nowhere in sight. To his credit, I never did see him, but as we prepared to get under way several hours later, I swear I saw a pair of binoculars peeking through the bulrushes on the shore.

What a great week we had. Dahleen was enthusiastic and willing to try anything. Like most women, before she did anything she wanted to know what was going to happen and why. So before we attempted any maneuver on the water, we discussed it at length at the dock. The only time I took the wheel was when Dahleen went below to practice making radio calls. Otherwise, she drove the boat.

We practiced docking from every angle, starting with the easier landings on t-heads and moving up to trickier ones in her own slip. And we did it over and over while guys on nearby boats looked on with curiousity.

By the end of the week we'd covered all the topics that you'll find in this book. We only had time for a cursory introduction to some, but it gave Dahleen a taste for all that's involved in being a competent mariner.

For her "final exam" I planned a special outing. Dahleen, at the helm, passed the first challenge by capably departing her slip. We headed south, where she faced the test of going through a drawbridge. Dahleen called the bridge operator on the radio to request an opening. Then she practiced the "backing and filling" maneuver she'd learned to hold the boat in place in the tricky currents while waiting for the drawbridge to open. Then she scored big points by skillfully powering through the bridge and using the radio to thank the operator for the opening.

Using her new piloting skills, Dahleen followed the navigation aids, comparing them with those on the chart by the helm, and guided us to our mid-term destination, a lovely waterfront café downriver. Never having been there before, she prepared fenders and dock lines, then landed the boat at the restaurant's pier. After properly securing the boat with bow, stern, and spring lines, we went ashore for lunch, but it wasn't yet time for a celebratory mimosa—she still had to get us home. The return trip was a breeze as Dahleen repeated the morning's activities to get us safely back to her homeport.

The final test was getting into the slip. We'd gone in and out repeatedly all week, but this time she needed to back the boat in for some upcoming maintenance. This was a maneuver we hadn't practiced, but as with everything else, we discussed it thoroughly beforehand. The theory was the same. She now had the skills. All she needed was the confidence, and Dahleen had no shortage of that.

As if she'd been handling a boat all her life, Dahleen made a wide turn down the fairway and aligned the boat with her slip. With an audience of two young dockhands standing by, she backed that boat in between the pilings with no need for the fenders she'd hung. Unfettered by macho "standards of conduct," the two of us hooted, hollered, hugged, and high-fived.

She had graduated with honors. My student was absolutely radiant—glowing with pride and a newfound self-confidence.

Dahleen later wrote to thank me:

> *I had so much fun I can't express it enough. Greg was jealous about the special instruction, but very happy for me. I wanted him to know that he can count on me if needed.*
>
> *I was like the average woman out there: intimidated in a field that was foreign to me. Now I feel I can work as a team with Greg and I can even critique our mistakes and successes. Whereas before I felt he was giving all the commands because he knew more than I did, now I can share and grow with him.*

The next time Dahleen went to Charleston, she and Greg took the boat a few miles offshore. The wind picked up to 15 knots and the boat heeled with the toe rail in the water—all with Dahleen at the helm. She told me it was an exhilarating experience. When Greg reefed the main and genoa, she understood why. As the wind changed directions and they trimmed the sails, she understood why. She thoroughly enjoyed herself and experienced the intense pride of being a real part of the crew. She couldn't wait to get back out and go sailing again.

Now that's a great attitude.

These days when Greg and Dahleen take their boat out, she takes the initiative, rather than waiting for someone to tell her what to do. And what person likes to be told what to do—especially by their partner?

Dahleen was lucky. She has a supportive husband who was self-confident enough not to feel threatened by her increased skill and knowledge. He understood that if Dahleen was going to share his dream, she needed to take on a bigger role on board.

Not every husband is as understanding as Greg. The problem is, knowledge is power. If a woman knows as much as or more than her partner does, there's a chance he may feel threatened. Unfortunately, there are some men who, to avoid criticism or competition, would rather their partner not learn more about boating.

My first boating partner was like that, but I didn't realize it at the time. I had grown up on powerboats and was new to sailing. Without ever saying so, he allowed me to believe that docking was extremely difficult. There was obviously great risk of damage to the boat if anyone but he were to attempt to take it in or out of the slip, so he always did it. I dutifully performed my role as line handler, more worried about being yelled at for doing something wrong than watching to learn how he maneuvered the boat. Unless we were in open water, he never offered to give me the helm, and it never occurred to me to ask.

Now I know better.

My husband spent his career driving Navy ships. As captain, one of his responsibilities was training junior officers. He thought nothing of letting me take our boat in and out of tight places. In fact, he insisted on it. I had no idea just how supportive he was until he left me.

Allow me to explain.

We were living in the Seattle area, where I was enjoying a great Navy assignment as the commanding officer of a personnel unit. Knowing it would soon be time for me to transfer, Ty found a new job in the other Washington . . . D.C. He started work four months before I was able to join him, leaving me rattling around our empty house on the weekends. I complained to Ty about my restlessness during one of our long nightly phone calls.

He replied, "Why don't you get a couple of girlfriends and take the boat out on Saturday?"

I was so shocked I almost dropped the receiver. Was he for real? At the time, we had a Freedom 36 sloop. She was a great boat—fast, and fun to sail. She was also the most expensive vessel either of us had ever owned.

"Take the boat out without you?" I asked.

"Sure. Why not?"

Why . . . because he was the captain. Why . . . because I'd never even considered such a preposterous idea. Why, because yes, it was our boat, but it was really his boat. You know what I mean?

I think you do.

I've experienced both sides of the supportive partner coin, and I now know how important it is to take the initiative if encouragement is lacking. It takes courage to ask or even insist on taking more responsibility, but it's worth it.

Don't let someone else's ego stop you from learning all you can about boating. Don't let your own history hold you back from enjoying your boat as much as your partner. Like Dahleen, no matter how little you know at this moment, aim to be on equal footing with the captain or aim to be the (co-) captain.

It's time to expand your horizons.

There's no denying that there are jobs aboard a boat that are traditionally "pink jobs" and those that are "blue jobs." The pink jobs are those such as cooking, cleaning, provisioning, and line handling. Blue jobs are docking, anchoring, and maintaining and fixing things. Some tasks, such as navigating, fall into a gray area that could go either way.

I'm a firm believer that there should be no gender-specific jobs aboard a boat. Rather, tasks should be taken on by those who enjoy them the most. Skill will come with experience. Many jobs, like docking and line handling, which require that skills be kept sharp, can and should be shared fifty-fifty.

Two of the most well-known sailors among cruising couples are Lin and Larry Pardey. They've been sailing together for over forty years and share their vast knowledge through a series of excellent books and DVDs/videos.[2] What stands out about the Pardeys is their obvious love of the water and the equality with which they share all responsibilities. It's the type of partnership all boating couples should strive for.

Don't automatically assume that you won't like doing certain tasks. Many times we dislike doing something simply because we don't know enough about it to enjoy it.

Ty used to do all the maintenance aboard *Liberty*. I didn't enjoy maintenance because my role was always the "gofer," and half the time I felt as if he were speaking a foreign language. You know: "Suzanne, go-fer the flex-head socket wrench with the whozzifratz on the end." This was usually followed by, "No, not that whozzifratz; the short one."

One day I decided I was tired of being the gofer. We'd bought a new water pump to replace an older, noisier model, and I told Ty that I wanted to install it. His eyebrows rose predictably, but then he smiled and said, "Great! Have at it."

---

[2] The Pardeys' books, DVDs, and videos are available from Paradise Cay Publications, Inc. www.paracay.com

I opened the box, unfolded the instructions, and took a look at what I'd gotten myself into.

Ladies, the secret is out: There is no magic involved in repairing and fixing things.

Replacing the pump required detaching the old one from its hoses and, after making sure all power to the unit was turned off, cutting the wires. The new one wasn't the same model, so I had to drill a couple of holes for the mounting screws. Reattaching the hoses wasn't easy in the small space, but once they were on, it was a breeze to screw the hose clamps in place.

Across the room Ty sat quietly reading his newspaper. I sensed an occasional glance in my direction, but he was under strict orders not to give me any pointers. If I needed help, I'd ask for it. And you can bet I wasn't going to ask for it unless water started gushing into the galley.

Connecting and crimping wires was another trick I'd learned through years of gofering. Like most jobs on a boat, some of the connections required me to contort my body into positions it wasn't meant to go into. I nicked my fingers and got a cramp in my leg. I took these as evidence that I was doing things right and vowed not to curse aloud.

Everything looked good, so I turned on the power and flipped the breaker. I hope that you, too, will soon experience the pride and satisfaction I felt when that new pump chugged to life. I'd done it! I'd installed a water pump from start to finish.

If you're not ready to take on a project by yourself, find a job that needs to be done and do it with your partner, with both of you contributing equal effort. Having discovered how much fun it was to do something mechanical, I wanted to help install a pair of winches we had bought for our cockpit. Knowing there would be steps I wouldn't know how to do, I made Ty a deal. He would install the port winch, and I would install the starboard one. He would do everything on his side one step ahead of me, then I would repeat it on my side.

It didn't take long before I ran into a glitch. The old winches had been on the boat for twenty-five years. They were bolted on so tightly that I couldn't budge them. Here we go, I thought, hindered right from the start because I'm the "weaker sex." That's when Ty taught me a trick of the trade. By putting a long screwdriver through the round end of the wrench, I was able to apply enough torque to break the nut free. I didn't have to be a big he-man to do the job, after all. Once again, it wasn't magic; it was plain old mechanical advantage.

There were multiple steps involved in installing my winch, but I learned something with every one. More than anything, I learned how much fun it was to be doing rather than watching and fetching.

Sound good to you?

Dahleen discovered the pride of understanding how things work. I learned that maintenance is not just a man's domain. You can enjoy the satisfaction of doing things aboard your boat that you've never done before. If you have a supportive partner, that's great. If not, now's the time to take a deep breath and have a little chat.

In either case, explain to your man that it's your boat, too, and you want to enjoy it as much as he does. To do so, you'd like to try some things you haven't done before. Whether it's fixing something, taking the helm, or plotting your course, you'll earn big payback when you take on a larger role aboard your vessel. Pride, self-confidence, and fun are the "feel-good" rewards. Even more important is the increased safety that will result from your participation.

Take tiny baby steps or jump right in with a giant leap for womankind. Like so many things in life, you won't know what you're missing until you push yourself beyond your comfort zone and try on a new role.

4

Safety First

In the last chapter, you read how I responded when my husband suggested I take our boat out without him. Assuming your partner were confident enough to make a similar offer, how would you have reacted?

Do I hear laughter?

I hope not, because this is actually a very serious issue. If you don't feel that you're capable of handling your boat on your own, you may be endangering not just yourself, but anyone else aboard your boat and the vessel itself.

The website www.ussailing.org lists over one hundred crew-overboard case histories that are real attention-grabbers. The most tragic are those in which a clueless crew member, not knowing how to handle the boat or the safety equipment, watches in horror as his or her partner floats away.

One story in particular tells of a woman whose husband fell overboard within sight of land. She was unable to maneuver the vessel and quickly lost sight of him. The distraught woman drifted around on the boat for three days until a passerby asked if she needed assistance. A check of the equipment on board showed a perfectly good VHF radio that could have been used to initiate a search days earlier, but the woman didn't even know how to make a basic distress call.

There's no excuse for that.

The time that woman needed assistance was when she and her husband first bought the boat. Instead of merely going along for the ride, she should have been working from the start to become as competent a sailor as her husband. She should have known how to drive the boat, learning basic maneuvering in forward and reverse, as well as starting and stopping the engine. She should have practiced docking until she was confident she could get in and out of a slip. She should have checked out the VHF, learning how to turn it on and off and how to make a distress call. She should have learned what the numbers on the GPS mean and how to read them over a radio. She should also have practiced plotting those same numbers on a chart, knowing exactly where she was at any time, able to find her way safely home.

There could be a number of reasons why the victim's wife never learned these basic yet vital skills. Like many first mates, she may have been quite content to be a potted plant on the poopdeck, and her husband may have been happy to leave her there. She may never have shown an interest in learning how to operate anything other than the stove. He may not have gone out of his way to expand her horizons.

Don't let that happen to you. Later in this book we'll review all the basic skills you should master to safely handle your boat. But don't just read about them. Put them to use and practice until you're comfortable with them.

Become familiar with all the safety equipment on your boat. Know where fire extinguishers and flotation devices are so you can grab them in an instant. Practice "what-if" drills on a regular basis. Ask yourself:

- "What if we hit a rock? What steps would I take?"

• "What if there were a fire in the galley? Do I know how to use the extinguisher?"

• "What if someone fell overboard today? What's the first thing I'd do? And the second . . ."

And so forth. What-if drills allow you to review every possible emergency scenario you can think of before it happens. The greater the detail you create, the better. These mental dress-rehearsals help you identify those areas you're unsure about and show you what skills you need to brush up on. They give you the confidence of knowing that should anything go wrong aboard your boat, you'll know what to do.

If you don't know what the appropriate response would be to a particular crisis, find out now, while there's no urgency. If you realize you couldn't navigate your way home using a chart, or make a radio call, or dock the boat, learn how. Discuss these things with your partner to ensure you agree on the appropriate actions.

There are people out there who do what-if drills for a living. They're called actuaries, and are employed by insurance companies. These brainy mathematicians are experts at calculating risk. They predict misfortune based on statistics.

As a boater, you don't need a statistician to tell you that boats can be dangerous. There's a reason they call that thing on a sailboat the "boom." Rather than consulting actuarial tables, I rely on the simple Law of Murphy: "If anything can go wrong, it will—at the most inopportune time."

Unfortunately, even knowing that Murphy rules, some boaters underestimate their environment. Figuring that the chance of something going wrong is slim, they adopt the hazardous attitude that "it's not gonna happen to me."

Tragedy can be minimized or avoided altogether through a process called risk analysis. That's an actuary's fancy term for "look before you leap." Risk analysis is as simple as assessing a situation or action in advance, thinking through all the possible mishaps that could occur as a result of that action, and taking appropriate measures before trouble arises.

You can never be too careful on a boat. As long as a risk exists, no matter how unlikely a mishap seems, it pays to err on the side of caution.

You may not be aware of it, but you practice risk analysis every day. Often the precautions we take are so habitual that we don't give them a second thought. Before you cross the street, you look left and right because you know there's a danger of being hit by a car. When you leave the house, you make sure the iron's unplugged and the coffee pot's turned off.

A boat's electrical and mechanical systems are more complex and demanding than in a house; the nautical environment is more unforgiving. Unless you've grown up on boats, many of the steps for safety afloat are not second nature. This is where risk analysis needs to become a conscious and deliberate process.

Take through-hulls as an example. These are the holes in your boat that are supposed to be there: the ones that let the waste water from your sink and head drain to the sea, or the one that brings in cooling water for your inboard engine. Do you know the location of every one of the through-hulls on your boat? You should.

Most home-owners don't worry about the plumbing in their houses when they leave for a day. I doubt you close the valve at the base of your toilet before you go out to dinner. But boats are different. They all have at least a couple of inlets and outlets which, if not properly attended, could ruin your whole day.

Your number one goal aboard your boat should always be to keep the people on the inside and the water on the outside.

The cautious boater will first assess the risk presented by the holes in her hull that are supposed to be there: a hose could pop off the connector to the through-hull, a sea cock could freeze in place or have metal failure. Would you know how to react if that happened? Do you know how to prevent it in the first place?

Once an element of risk has been determined, you should do everything necessary to minimize or eliminate the hazard. On a boat, this includes such things as inspecting your through-hulls each time the boat is hauled, using high quality all-stainless steel double hose clamps on all hoses and routinely checking them, tying an appropriately sized wooden plug with a lanyard to each through-hull, and closing all through-hulls every time you leave the boat.

The latter suggestion may seem extreme. Admittedly, it's a pain to get down on your hands and knees, lift the floorboards, and open and close the valves. But it all comes down to your level of comfort with risk taking. The risk is there. How much of a gambler are you?

Do you turn off all electrical switches when the boat is unattended? How many mooring lines do you use? Do you give your passengers a safety briefing before getting under way? Do you have one or two anchors at the ready?

I once saw a boat careening down a narrow channel in 40 knots of wind. No one was aboard. A Good Samaritan jumped onto the bow from a small powerboat and began pulling in the anchor chain. When he got to the end, there was no anchor on it. The captain hadn't inspected the shackle for wear, nor had he analyzed the risk of having only one anchor. Now it was on the bottom, somewhere upstream.

Risk analysis can be applied to almost everything you do, and it only takes seconds.

• Before stepping out of the cockpit on a windy day, stop and assess the situation. Are the decks slick? Is the boat heeling so much that you should step out on the windward side instead of the leeward? If you're on a sailboat, is there danger of the boom jibing and hitting you?

• Before you jump in the water to go for a swim or check the boat's hull, stop and think about unseen dangers. How deep is the water? Diving head first into water that's too shallow can break your neck. Another possible peril is invisible: When your boat is in a marina, stray electrical current in the water can be deadly. Turn off the 110v power at the pier to your boat and those on both sides of you.

• Before you get under way, listen to the weather channel on your VHF radio.

The list goes on and on, but it all comes down to learning about your boat and its systems so you know what things can present a danger if not looked after.

On your boat, there should always be at least two passengers: you, and Prudence. Prudence is a handy gal to have along, but she can be mighty bossy at times—dictatorial, in fact. You know . . . Prudence dictates that you always put safety first. She keeps you out of trouble.

What's your boat worth? Every vessel has a dollar value assigned by an insurer. But what's it worth to you? Boats have a strong emotional value that's impossible to quantify. You may have a lot invested in your boat—not just money, but sweat equity as well. With an investment like that, it's foolhardy and dangerous to let complacency creep aboard. Underestimating Murphy's Law can have tragic consequences.

When risks seem low, it's human nature to ask, "What are the chances that'll happen to me?" It's even riskier to disregard the odds.

When it comes to safety, you can never have too much of a good thing.

5

The Fear Factor

Women are worriers. I hate to stereotype, but I think that's a fair statement. We fret and stew over all kinds of things that men don't give a second thought about.

It's one thing to worry. A little extra concern ensures that things get done and that details don't fall through the cracks. But fear is another thing altogether.

Fear can be debilitating. It can cause you to panic and freeze—to be unable to take appropriate action when needed. On a boat, where sometimes you have to react quickly in a crisis, that can be a very bad thing.

Even in its milder forms, fear feels pretty lousy. I'm sure you know that awful, panicky feeling when your heart speeds up and adrenaline rushes painfully through your veins, turning your arms and legs to jelly. Who needs that?

Actually, we all do. Those uncomfortable symptoms are God's way of telling you, "Take action, or get out of here now."

Yes, it's the old fight-or-flight syndrome. If it weren't for the discomfort we experience when our brain senses a threat—sometimes before we're even aware we're in danger—we might end up with far more problems than mere rapid heartbeats and squiggly limbs.

Because fear feels so unpleasant, we women often avoid potentially scary situations. This would include times when we're not in control, when we don't understand how everything around us works, and when we're not totally comfortable in our surroundings.

Like on a boat, maybe?

Sailing and boating expose you to a unique environment. On the water you face ever-changing conditions and experiences that landlubbers never have to deal with. These include a host of things which some may find frightening, such as heeling, big waves, big ships, bad weather, and being out of sight of land. Some women fear the unknown and not knowing how to react in emergencies. Others are afraid of falling overboard, swimming with sharks, and drowning.

Come to think of it, who wouldn't fear these things?

But don't worry. There are ways of dealing with frightening situations, whether real or imagined.

Yes, imagined. Even worse than panicking when things have gone haywire is making yourself miserable worrying about things that might never happen. Unfortunately, you get the same physical sensations from an imaginary situation as from a real one. This is called "anticipatory anxiety." If you were to analyze what's going on in your brain, you'd discover that what you're actually afraid of is the feeling of being afraid.

Now, how useful is that? What purpose does it serve? None. It only causes you to pass up things that might turn out to be a lot of fun.

You'll recall from the discussion about attitude that only you control your thoughts. Well, the same holds true for fear. Distress is not mandatory. Panicking in scary situations is not a requirement. I'm here to tell you that it's possible to remain calm even in the most frightful incident you can imagine. Not easy, but possible.

If something on your boat scares you or makes you uncomfortable, whether you find yourself in an actual hazardous situation or you're suffering from anticipatory anxiety, you deal with it the same way. The solution involves a three-step process that puts you immediately back in control: You must recognize, accept, and release.

1. The moment you experience the fight or flight syndrome, recognize that what you're feeling is a perfectly normal physiological response. It's your body's built-in alert system that is impossible to turn off (and you wouldn't want to).

2. Acknowledge and accept your body's reaction as a useful tool, and recognize that you have the power to make your fears disappear.

3. Release your fear, now that it has served its purpose of alerting you, and deal with the situation.

Here are some quick and easy ways of releasing your fear once you recognize it. To save you the trouble, I have personally tested each of these in actual fear-inducing situations and can guarantee their effectiveness:

• Talk to yourself. There's nothing like the voice of reason to calm your nerves. You've taken the time to learn how your boat works (at least you will after you've finished this book). You've done your what-if drills and visualized how to handle things. Tell yourself, "I can handle this. I know what to do. I don't need to be afraid. I'm just going to deal with this situation and learn from it."

• Smile. It takes real effort to be afraid when you're smiling. There's some kind of physiological connection between the muscles in your mouth and your brain that makes you instantly feel better when you break into a grin. If you're a doctor, maybe you can explain it to me some day. All I know is that it works.

One summer we were sailing off the coast of Newfoundland. The wind was forecast to decrease from 25 knots to a pleasant 15. Instead, it increased to 42 knots. I'd never heard such horrendous howling, and the boat was rocking like one of those playground horses on a spring. My fight-or-flight syndrome was tugging at my jacket, saying,

"Hey, Suzanne, let's get out of here," but there was no place to run. So rather than curling up in a little ball, I stood there at the helm with a big old grin pasted on my face.

Ty poked his head up in the cockpit, took one look at me and said, "I can't tell whether you're scared out of your wits or having the time of your life." And you know . . . after a few minutes, neither could I. Because the smile had taken the edge off my fear, I was able to see that we weren't in any real danger. I realized that all the rolling was mighty uncomfortable, but everything was under control. The strong wind was new to me, but I was managing it. Yes, I was successfully handling a gale, and I was proud of myself. That's when I started to...

• Sing. I'm perfectly serious. Singing is a great distraction and psychologically works along the same lines as smiling. Be aware that when you're truly agitated you may have trouble remembering the lyrics to even your favorite song. That's ok. Just be sure to choose something upbeat and make up the words as you go if you have to. During that Newfoundland gale, I belted out the Star Spangled Banner, and it did the trick just fine.

• Act as if you're not afraid. This is especially important if you are the captain or are hosting guests, because everyone aboard will take their cue from you. In any case, because your mind and body are connected, act calm and you'll feel calm.

• Practice deep breathing. All those yogis can't be wrong.

• Pray. It works miracles.

While you're at it, come up with a list of positive affirmations about yourself and your boat. Put these in your back pocket and pull them out from time to time. Repeat them frequently. Even if you don't necessarily believe them, simply telling yourself the same thing over and over will condition your thoughts. This will go a long way towards curing that anticipatory anxiety we talked about.

Here are some helpful boating affirmations:

"I trust my skills and knowledge to help me through any crisis."

"I trust my boat to get me safely where I'm going."

"When I become aware of fear, I acknowledge it, then release it."

"I have a plan to deal with fear."

"When I'm in a tense situation, I breathe deeply and deal with it."

"Fear is an unnecessary waste of time."

"I trust that God is always guiding and protecting me."

"I am brave."

Even if you're the original Chicken Little, if you continue to repeat this type of affirmation, your mind won't know the difference. It will respond to what you tell it. So tell yourself only positive things and don't allow your fears to control you.

We get in the habit of reacting to situations the same way each time they occur. If your normal response to fright is to panic and throw your hands in the air, you may not know any other way to act. Again, it's not necessary to give in to your first feelings of fright. Those are just warning signs. You can make them go away. The three steps we just discussed take awareness and conscious action, but they put you immediately back in control.

The goal, however, is to prevent the fight or flight syndrome from occurring in the first place. You want to enjoy boating and look forward to going out on the water. And you want to do so safely. So learn everything you can about this great activity. Become a sponge. When you understand how things work and how they will respond to your actions, you won't be afraid to try them.

Get as much hands-on experience as you can. Don't just read and observe; get out there and practice what you learn. The more you do things on your boat yourself, the more confident you'll become. Push yourself beyond your comfort zone in tiny steps. Each time you work through something that makes you uneasy, you'll see that you're able to deal with it. The next time you're in a similar situation, it'll be a piece of cake. You'll look back at things that used to scare you and smile.

Practice prevention. This involves that process of risk analysis we talked about—thinking things through in advance and asking yourself what could go wrong. Of course, you have to know what the potential dangers are in order to avoid them, which takes you right back to education. It's just not smart to play ostrich when it comes to boats. To be safe, you should learn everything you can. Know how to predict bad weather. Become a better swimmer. Learn what it takes to keep from falling overboard. Keep those scary situations at bay and fear not.

Education, experience, and prevention: these are the keys to serenity at sea. Go back to the list of potentially frightening things I mentioned at the beginning of this chapter and you'll see what I mean.

Take heeling, for example. When you're a novice sailor, it can be pretty disconcerting to find yourself and the platform on which you're riding leaning over at a precarious angle. It's unnatural. If your car did that when rounding a curve, it could tip over, right? Well, unless you know something about sailboat design and the way sails work, you could easily assume that your boat might do the same.

A little education, however, will teach you that a boat's keel and ballast work to overcome the pressure put on the sails by the wind. As the boat heels farther, some of the wind will actually spill out the top of the sail. Then the keel takes over and brings the boat back upright. Little Sunfish and sailing dinghies do tip over because they have neither ballast nor keels. Their crews expect to go swimming. Larger keelboats are designed to return to an upright position, even if the boat rolls 90 degrees or more.

Knowing that makes a huge difference. That knowledge helps ease the fear while you get out there on the water and repeatedly experience your boat heeling over. When it leans so far that the toe rail is in the water, you'll see that it's not tipping over. That's what sailboats do. In fact, heeling is kind of fun. It's what makes sailing so exhilarating once you get over your fears. It's just a matter of getting used to the feeling and understanding the forces at work.

If you're not really into rail-in-the-water sailing, practice prevention. Apply your newfound knowledge of sail trim and de-power the sails until you're heeling at a nice, comfortable fifteen degrees. If you study boat design a little more, you'll learn that fifteen degrees of heel is usually more efficient than leaning over so far that you have to hold on. For those of you married to Speed Racer, you may want to share that tidbit of information with him.

How about another example of using education and experience to deal with fear?

I was sailing out of sight of land one day when a large tanker came across the horizon. Our two vessels were on reciprocal courses. That means he was headed right for me, but I couldn't tell which side we were going to pass each other on. If in doubt, vessels should pass port to port. On this particular day, the seas were big, and I wasn't sure if the ship could see us or not. I tried raising him on the radio, but there was no response.

This was in the days before I learned how to handle my fears, so my instinctive reaction was to panic. I envisioned us turning the wrong way to avoid the ship and ending up right in its path—anticipatory anxiety that did nothing to help me handle the situation. As the ship got closer and closer, I paced around the cockpit like a rat in a cage. I felt trapped and terrified. My husband, on the other hand, was the picture of serenity. Because he had had so much more time at sea than I, he could tell on which side of us the ship would pass just by looking at it. He assured me the ship would pass well clear of us, and it did.

The physical sensation of fear and the feeling of helplessness during that incident was awful. I never wanted to feel that way again. I knew there'd be plenty more encounters with ships in my future as a cruiser, and I didn't care to repeat my previous embarrassing performance. I had to face my fears head on.

Luckily, education and experience came to my rescue.

I bought a book on collision avoidance and read it from cover to cover. It spelled out which way to turn depending on the angle of approach of a ship. To reinforce what I read, Ty and I sat down and discussed every conceivable scenario in which we might meet a larger vessel and how we should respond. The biggest help was learning how to use our radar to track ships' movements.

Once I had some knowledge under my belt, I put it to use on the water. At first, in spite of my preparations, that old fight or flight syndrome kicked in when I'd see the outline of a ship miles away. My brain and body were still conditioned to react that way. Making a conscious effort, I acknowledged that it was ok for my body to react that way. Then I released the fear. I talked to myself, reasoning that I no longer had to be afraid because I had studied collision avoidance and knew what to do.

Once I'd let go of my fear, I dealt with the situation by tracking the ship with the radar and maneuvering as necessary to avoid coming too close. Each time thereafter that I successfully handled an encounter with a ship, my confidence grew. Today, I look forward to seeing ships at sea. On a long passage they spice up my turn at the helm and provide a welcome challenge.

It's a good thing I faced my fears, because crossing the shipping lanes off the coast of Portugal I had ten large ships on my radar screen at once. They were all within six miles of us and going in various directions. Was I scared? Not the slightest bit. I actually enjoyed working out that little puzzle. What a difference from the Nervous Nellie I'd been before I learned the secret to controlling fear.

It will work the same way for you. Learn all you can about your boat, get as much experience as possible, and practice prevention. Be aware that you control your fears, and go forth with confidence.

Yeah, sure, you're thinking. That's really going to help with those truly scary boating things like falling overboard, swimming with sharks, and drowning.

Actually, it is.

The risk of falling overboard is always present on a boat. But so is the danger of being hit by a car when you walk down the street or go for a drive. You can't worry about those sorts of things all the time or you'd drive yourself crazy. All you can do is learn what the dangers are and practice prevention.

One of the best ways to keep from falling overboard is to maintain one hand for yourself and one for the boat. This means that you always hold onto something as you move about, because you never know when the boat may lurch. You wear a safety harness when conditions warrant. You wear proper footwear when the deck is wet. You learn how to do a man-overboard recovery and you practice it, just in case.

No matter what the situation, with enough experience you'll become more and more comfortable in the boat environment and will be able to put your fears to rest. Get smart, and watch your fears melt away. The less frightened you are, the more fun you'll have. Each time you successfully handle something that frightens you, you'll emerge stronger and more confident.

In Ken Blanchard's best-selling book, *Who Moved My Cheese?* he raises the wonderfully thought-provoking question, "What would you do if you weren't afraid?"

I hope that in your case, you'd go boating.

6

Looking Good

If you've read any of John Gray's outstanding books, you know that men and women come from different planets.[3] I always suspected this was true, but it's been proven to me repeatedly aboard my boat. I'm talking about the very dissimilar way men and women react to trying new things.

When faced with something they've never done before, men tend to jump right in and give it a try. Women want to know how or why things work before they try things. They want to know exactly what's going to happen if and when they do something.

Once again, it's all about fear. But this time I'm not talking about the kind that makes you all nervous and jittery. This kind of fear doesn't cause actual physical symptoms. It's not quite so immediate, nor as uncomfortable, but it still holds you back from fully enjoying boating.

I'm talking about the very human fear of looking bad. No, ladies, I don't mean having a bad hair day. I'm talking about being afraid of looking stupid, dumb, ignorant, or silly.

---

[3] Gray, John. *Men Are From Mars, Women Are From Venus*. Harper Collins, New York, 1992.

The interesting thing is that men and women share the same potential for looking bad when they try something new, but for a man, it seems the desire to accept a challenge or solve a problem outweighs the need to look good.

Here's how I've seen this in action: We invite a couple to join us sailing. Neither of them has ever been on a boat before. They're equally happy and excited to be out on the water. We raise the sails and head into open water. I turn to the man and ask, "Would you like to take the wheel?" Without hesitation, he jumps up and says, "Sure!"

Now, sailing a boat is not like driving a car. Some people are real naturals at the helm. Others take a little while to catch on. Let's say our friend takes the wheel and leaves a wake like a snake instead of a nice, straight line. No matter. He stands there at the helm with a huge smile on his face—not to cover up his fear, but because he's having a blast.

Once our male guest gets his hands on the helm it's hard to pry them off. We want to give his wife equal time, however, so I turn to the woman and ask, "Would you like a turn?"

This is where the planetary differences show up. She invariable shrinks back, shakes her head nervously, gives a little wave-off with her hand, and says, "That's ok."

Her husband is all too happy to keep driving, and she's happy to just sit there. After all, she might break something, or do something wrong, or look dumb . . . .

This is a prime example of not knowing what you're missing unless you give it a try.

Sure, they both enjoyed themselves, but who do you think had more fun? Who had the greater adventure? A friend of mine described adventure as something enjoyable that involves participation and an element of risk. The woman participated only by sitting in the cockpit. She took no risks. The man participated fully by taking the wheel. He risked trying something new. He enjoyed a real adventure.

The woman will go to work on Monday and she might tell her friends she went sailing over the weekend. For sure, the man will stand around the water fountain and brag to all his buddies about how he sailed a boat. Passive vs. active.

When it comes to trying something new, men just jump right in, even if they're a little unsure of themselves. They like to solve problems. That's why they won't ask for directions. They'd rather drive around the block four times and find their way on their own. Women prefer to go straight to their destination the first time and look good.

When you read this chapter title, you thought I was going to teach you some beauty secrets for sea, didn't you? No way. Some of my worst moments in the mirror have been after a day of being out in the wind and sun. I may have looked like a wild woman, but I had a great time.

No, you won't find any beauty advice here, nor will you find tips for the galley or lessons on how to stow things. You can find that plenty of other places. The purpose of this book is to get you to step beyond your self-imposed limits and take on a bigger role aboard your boat. The purpose of this chapter is to help you realize how fear of looking bad can keep you from becoming completely engaged.

If you're going to fully enjoy your boat, you need to be on the lookout for the female tendency to not take risks. If you have the chance to take the helm, take it every time. If you see an opportunity to try something you've never done before, grab it.

When I was little, my older brother used to say, "Suzy, don't be a ninny." I never heard anyone else being called a ninny, but I sure seemed to be one. Luckily, I became much more self-assured as I grew up. One day not too long ago I saw a great poster with a boat bravely riding across the waves. The woman at the helm was smiling and having a great time. When I read the caption at the bottom, I could hardly believe my eyes. It read: "No ninnies".

Can you put yourself in that poster? If not, make it a goal. When you hold back from trying new things, you deprive yourself of having fun and growing.

We women need to get over this hang-up about looking bad. Don't be a ninny. Next time you go out on your boat, try something new. Go ahead and ask questions first so you know what to expect, then give it a go.

The truth is, nothing looks as good as self-confidence.

PART II

The Basics

7

Learning the Ropes

To become proficient in most hobbies or sports you study a single set of rules, then practice the related skills. Take tennis as an example. You learn the vocabulary, scoring, and how to play the game, then you spend the rest of your time perfecting your serve and returning the ball.

Seamanship is a whole different ball game. There's quite a bit more to learn than what "fifteen-love" and "advantage" mean. The rules in boating cover a variety of complex topics such as navigation, meteorology, electronics, and communications. Hands-on proficiency is required in diverse skills that include tying knots, coiling lines, maneuvering a vessel, and using tools.

What I'm trying to say without scaring you off is that when it comes to boating, there's a lot to learn.

Your basic books on seamanship cover a whole list of topics. Each of these is complex enough to merit an entire book of its own, and believe me, they're out there. The waterline on our boat is at least an inch lower than it should be, thanks to our library of subject-specific nautical books.

With so much to learn, where do you start and how do you ever learn it all?

You start anywhere you'd like, because it's all important. And don't expect to know everything after a few weeks of intense study. You can go boating for years and still discover new things every time you get under way. There'll be times you'll go out when the water will be calm and the winds light. The next time it could be gusty and rough. Each situation will require you to analyze tides and current, rig lines and fenders a particular way for leaving and returning to port, and handle your boat accordingly.

Mother Nature will continually throw pop quizzes to keep you on your toes. But don't let that discourage you. The ever-changing environment of the water is what keeps boating interesting.

When you're new to boating, the learning curve goes almost straight up. Most things are alien. It's like learning a foreign language. In fact, as you've surely discovered, boating has its own language, so in the material to follow, I've placed the chapter on nautical terminology right up front.

While the curve is steep, the things I'm going to share with you here will all be relevant, useful, and immediately applicable. Each time you get under way you'll have a chance to put some of what you've learned to use. Soon, skills that once seemed awkward will be second nature. Before you know it, you'll be swaggering around the docks like an old salt, at ease in the marine environment.

If there's so much to be learned, what do you need to know right now to be a safe and competent mariner? Why, all the information that follows, of course! This section of the book will give you an overview of the boating skills and knowledge with which you should be familiar—everything from how to properly use your VHF radio, to how to check the oil in your engine. Unlike more in-depth books like my favorite, *Chapman Piloting Seamanship & Small Boat Handling*, I won't describe polyconic projection charts, nor list the *International Regulations for the Prevention of Collisions at Sea* verbatim. That's not the purpose of this book.

My goal is to introduce you to each of the subject matter areas you'll likely encounter on your boat. I'll tell you what you should know about these things and why you should know it. Think of me as the teacher who says, "Class, there'll be a test on Friday. Everything you need to know can be found in chapters three to five of your textbook, but be sure you study thus and such . . . ."

I'll give you the basic nautical knowledge with which you should be most familiar. The real test comes when you get out there on the water.

As you read the following chapters, some areas will be completely new to you. Some will interest you more than others. The more intriguing ones may describe a subject you'd like to study more in depth. If so, consider making this your area of expertise on your boat, regardless of whether it's a pink or blue job.

For now, learn a little about each subject, then continue to expand your knowledge and skills. Even if you've only been a deck hand until now, it's never too late to become proficient in other areas. You may think you know the ropes, but there's a lot more to boating than simply handling the lines.

The information that follows will get you started. How far you go from here is up to you. There's no shortage of opportunities to study and grow, from books, to private lessons, to Power Squadron classes and nautical schools. I highly recommend women-only boating courses that foster a low-pressure, safe learning environment. By "safe" I mean that nobody's going to raise their voice if you don't do something exactly right.

No matter how you choose to improve your skills, remember that the more you learn, the more you'll enjoy boating and the greater your sense of security will be. Apply what you learn here on the water, and you'll be a more competent, a more confident, and a safer boater.

8

Nautical Terminology

Picture this scene: a woman is on a golf course. She has expensive clubs and is dressed just right. She approaches the tee, grips the driver perfectly, and swings. Wow. She must really know what she's doing, because she drives the ball straight down the fairway. Her ball soars through the air, and heads turn to watch. The woman sees other golfers off in the distance and wants to alert them, so she raises her hand to her mouth and calls out loudly, "Everybody DUCK!"

This woman just blew it. Every golfer knows that the proper way to alert others to a ball in the air is to call out, "Fore!" So in spite of being dressed right, having good equipment, and possessing excellent golfing skills, the lady has just exposed herself as an uninformed novice.

Like any sport, boating has its own language. Speak the lingo and you fit right in. That's why I put this chapter on nautical terminology first—salt your language with the right words, appropriately used, and you'll sound as if you've been around the waterfront awhile. Use the wrong terminology, and you might as well hang a sign around your neck with big, bold letters saying, "Landlubber."

Equally important as choosing the proper nautical term is pronouncing it correctly. For example, the main cabin in a boat is often referred to as a salon. For some reason, many boat ads and brochures spell this "saloon." Pronounce this word like some bar in the Wild West and you'll sound as if that's where you just came from.

I once gave a woman a lesson in tying knots. We concentrated on four that you'll learn about in the chapter on line handling. When we got to the bowline, she stopped me and asked, "Why did you pronounce that 'bó-lynn?'"

I shrugged my shoulders and said, "That's just the way everybody says it."

She then asked, "What if I pronounce it 'bo-line?'"

I smiled and said, "Then everybody will know you really don't know what you're talking about."

We laughed and got on with our lesson. About a week later I ran into the same woman and she put her hand on my arm. "I have to tell you something," she said. "I went home and showed my husband how I learned to tie a bowline."

"Was he impressed?" I asked.

"I guess so," she answered, "but he told me I was saying the word wrong, that it was pronounced 'bo-line.'"

I laughed, remembering our conversation. "What did you do?"

She held her head up proudly and announced, "I told him it was really bo-lynn, and that he was showing how ignorant he was by saying it wrong."

Maybe there's a reason men don't want us to get smarter about boats.

All humor aside, there's a far more important reason for using proper nautical terminology than simply to show you've done your homework. Using the correct words will allow you to speak precisely and get your point across promptly. This can save valuable seconds, which can often be crucial on a moving boat.

It's far quicker to shout, "Man overboard, starboard side!" than to have the following conversation:

"Oh my gosh. George just fell in the water!"

"Where?"

"On the right!"

"Is that your right or my right?"

On a boat, there is only one starboard—it's the right side of the boat when facing forward. No matter which way you or anyone else is looking or facing, starboard is always starboard. Use the proper nautical terms and eliminate confusion.

The list of words you'll learn here is not all-inclusive. It doesn't include more advanced terms you may never need, such as those used in boat construction. There are a few others that you'll pick up in the remaining chapters as I use them in context. The ones that follow are the most common boating terms, which should become as natural to you as using your own name.

Where, Exactly, Is It?

(Indicating Direction or Location)

Aft*[4] : Behind the boat; or, the back half of a boat.

- "I like to sleep in the aft cabin."
- "Be sure to look fore and aft for obstructions."

Ahead*: This means the same as in landlubber terms, but it's also used to indicate forward motion.

- "Come ahead slowly."
- "Where's that other boat? Up ahead."

Amidships: In the center of the boat.

- "The best place to sleep in comfort is amidships."
- "The mast is located amidships."

[4] "Landlubber Alert." Failure to use words marked with an asterisk will immediately identify you as a newbie.

Astern*: Behind.

- "There's a big ship astern of us."
- "Let's tow the dinghy astern."

Athwartships: Running from side to side.

- "The galley counter runs athwartships."
- "The dinette seat is set athwartships."

Beam*/Abeam: The side of a boat. Things you point out are "off the beam." (Also refers to how wide a boat is)

- "There's a pretty lighthouse off the port beam."
- "He's coming abeam of us now."

Below*/Belowdecks: Inside, particularly on a sailboat, which is usually accessed by going down a ladder.

- "Go below and check the chart."

Fore and aft: From the bow to the stern.

- "The keel runs fore and aft."

Forward*: Ahead, or "up front" on a boat.

- "Where did you leave the camera? Up forward."
- "The forward part of the boat is the bounciest."

Inboard: Toward the center part of the boat when facing fore and aft.

- "The sink is inboard of the stove."

Leeward: The side away from the wind. If the wind is blowing across the starboard side of your boat, the port side is the leeward side, and vice versa.

- "The boat's heeling a lot so you'd better not walk on the leeward side."

Outboard: Toward the sides of the boat, when facing fore and aft.

- "The ketchup is in the icebox—outboard, aft corner."

Port*: The left side of a boat, or on the left, when facing forward. If something is on the port side, you can also say that it's "to port."

- "Rig the fenders to port."
- "Rig the fenders on the port side."
- "We're going to tie up port-side-to."
- "Leave that red buoy to port."
- "Look at the dolphins on the port side."
- "Let's pass port to port."

Quarter: At the "back corner" of a boat, either port or starboard. Things are "off" the quarter.

- "I have a contact 100 yards off the starboard quarter."
- "Put the fishing line out off the port quarter."

Starboard*: The right side of a boat, or on the right, when facing forward. If something is on your starboard side, you can also say that it's "to starboard."

- "Let's dock with the finger pier to starboard."
- "Let's tie up starboard-side-to."
- "Let's dock with the finger pier on the starboard side."
- "Man overboard, starboard side!"
- "I'd like to overtake you on your starboard side."

Topside: On deck.

- "Come topside and watch the sunset."
- "I left my hat topside. Would you go get it?"

Windward: The side of the boat closest to the wind. If the wind is blowing across the starboard side of your boat, the starboard side is the windward side.

- "We don't want to anchor to windward of those rocks."

Putting these together, pretend you're standing topside, looking forward. If you were to point forward and indicate points around you in a complete circle, you would describe them as follows:

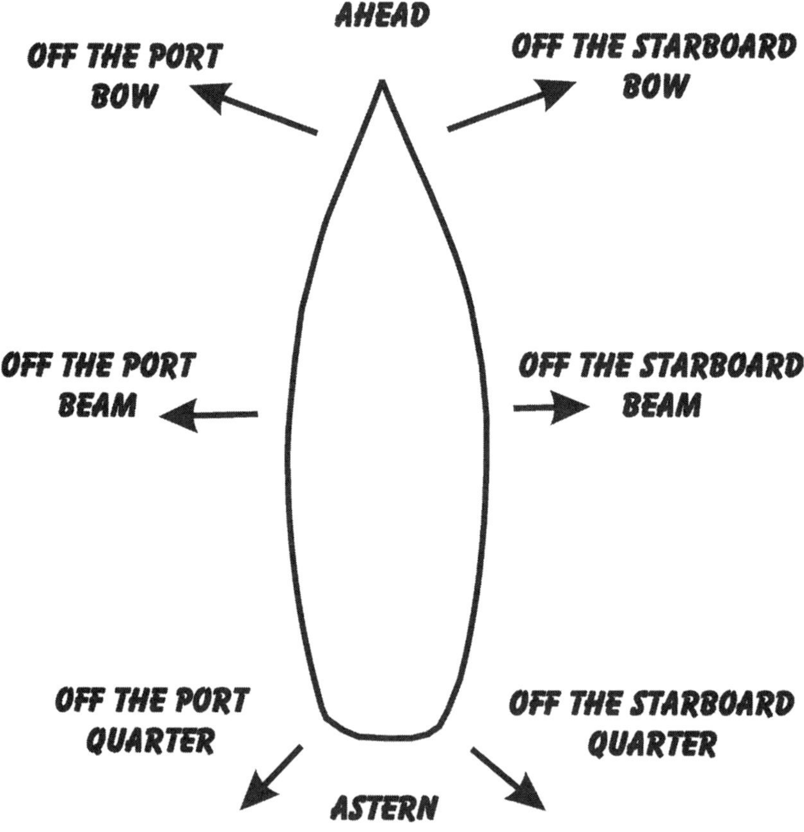

See how specific these nautical terms allow you to be? This is far better than pointing and saying, "Over there."

Describing Your Boat

Beam*: How wide the boat is (also refers to the side of a boat, when indicating direction).

- "What's your beam?" (Often asked by marina staff.)
- "Our beam is thirteen feet six inches."

Bow*: The pointy end of a boat.

- "Let's dock bow-in."
- "I'm looking at that ship bow-on."

Berth: A bunk where you sleep or a slip where you tie up your boat in a marina.

- "How many berths does your boat have?"
- "Where are you going to berth your boat for the winter?"

Bimini: A canvas awning over a cockpit or flybridge.

Bow Pulpit: The stainless steel rail around your bow.

Cabin*: A bedroom or stateroom.

- "Look how big the aft cabin is."

Cabin Sole/Sole: The floor belowdecks in a boat. The "deck" can be either topside or belowdecks, but the cabin sole is only below.

- "We put five coats of varnish on the cabin sole."
- "Our cabin sole is teak and holly."

Companionway: The "doorway" leading belowdecks, usually on a sailboat.

- "Their companionway ladder is really steep."
- "She forgot to slide back the companionway hatch, so she hit her head."

Dodger: A spray shield like a windshield, usually on a sailboat, with a clear plastic window.

Draft: How deep your boat is below the waterline. It's very important to know your boat's draft, or how much it draws, so you don't go aground.

- "What's your draft?" (Often asked by marina staff.)
- "She's a deep draft boat; she draws seven feet."

Fiddle: A rail across a shelf, counter, or table to keep books and other objects from falling off when a boat heels.

Flybridge: A steering station above the main deck on a powerboat.

Foul-weather gear: Waterproof clothing, hats, and boots worn by boaters. Also known as foulies and oilskins. A recent trend has been to sell navy blue foul-weather gear. Note that if you ever fall overboard while wearing foulies, you want to be seen. The best color for this purpose is bright yellow or red.

Freeboard: The height of the deck above the water.

- "That sailboat has a lot of freeboard. They must stay nice and dry."
- "Look how little freeboard that boat has."

Galley*: The kitchen.

- "I'm tired of being the galley slave."
- "If you can't stand the heat, get out of the galley."

Halyard: A rope (line) on a sailboat that is used to raise or lower a sail.

Hatch*: An overhead opening window.

- "Open that hatch and let some air in."
- "Be careful not to fall through the forward hatch while bringing in the anchor."

Head*: The bathroom, as well as the toilet itself. This term derived from sailing ships in the days before vessels had bathrooms. The toilet was nothing more than a plank across the bow, or head, of the boat.

- "Don't put anything in the head that you haven't already eaten."
- "The head on this boat includes a separate shower stall."
- "I need to use the head."

Ladder*: A stairway belowdecks on a boat. Also refers to a ladder for boarding a boat.

- "You might want to go down that ladder backwards."
- "Always hold on when you go down the ladder."

Lazarette: A locker at the stern of a boat that is usually flush with the deck.

Lifelines: The wires around the deck that keep the people on the inside.

- "It's better to hang fenders from the toe rail rather than from the lifelines."

Lines*: Ropes.

- "Please coil that line."
- "We need some more nylon line."

LOA: Length Over All. How long your boat is from bow to stern. Pronounce each individual letter, as in L-O-A.

- "What's your LOA?" (Often asked by marina personnel.)
- "Our LOA is forty-six feet."

Locker*: A closet or storage compartment.

- "This hanging locker is good for long coats."
- "Put that in the locker behind the settee."

Port*: A window on the sides of a boat, as opposed to a hatch, which is overhead.

- "Our boat has nine opening ports."
- "Look out the port on the port side—there's a whale."

Settee*: A couch, usually in the main salon. Often converts into a single berth.

Sheet*: A rope (line) on a sailboat that controls the shape of a sail.

- "Trim in the jib sheet." (See the chapter on sailing for more on this.)
- "Put a stopper knot in the end of that sheet."

Shrouds: The thick wires on a sailboat that hold the mast up from the sides, as opposed to "stays," which hold the mast up fore and aft.

Spreaders: The short "arms" attached to the mast that hold the shrouds away from the mast.

Stanchion: The vertical stainless steel rods around the deck that hold the lifelines.

Stays: The thick wires on a sailboat that hold the mast up fore and aft, as opposed to shrouds, which hold the mast up from the side.

Stern*: The round or flat end of a boat, as opposed to the bow or pointy end.

- "Let's dock stern-to."
- "Climb aboard at the stern ladder."

Stowage: Storage.

Transom: The vertical surface at the stern of a boat.

- "Should we put the boat's name on the side or across the transom?"
- "The swim platform is attached to the transom."

V-Berth: A cabin in the bow of a boat, usually triangular in shape.

Miscellaneous Terms

Ease: To let out a line little by little while maintaining tension.

- "Ease the jib sheet."
- "Since there's a lot of wind, gently ease that dock line while I put it around this piling."

Painter: A bow line on a dinghy.

Rode: The anchor line or chain.

- "He caught his rudder on that guy's anchor rode."

Scope: A ratio of length of anchor rode to the vertical distance from the bow of your boat to the bottom of the water .

- "How much scope should I put out?"
- "The bottom here is sticky mud. Should I use a scope of 5:1 or 7:1?"

Slack: To ease a line completely, letting all the strain off of it.

- "Slack the starboard bow line."

Yaw: A very uncomfortable motion in which a boat corkscrews between rolling side to side and rocking fore and aft.

Sundowners: Boating slang for "cocktails." Very good once you get to anchor.

- "The sun's below the yardarm. Time for a sundowner."

(Don't worry if you don't know what a yardarm is. It's an old sailing ship thing. Just refer to the recipe for Pain Killers in Chapter One and mix up a pitcher.)

9

THE RULES OF THE ROAD

Imagine you're driving down the Washington D.C. beltway, one of the busiest stretches of road in the United States. Cars enter the highway to your right from the on-ramps. Others zip up from behind and pass you. Still more cut across four lanes, whizzing past from right to left and left to right. Although you're alert, you're relatively relaxed, tooling along at the same high speed as everyone else.

Why? Because in spite of the density of traffic, it's all quite orderly. There's a set of rules governing how to drive, and for the most part, people around you are following them. Cars entering the highway know to yield to those already in the right lane. Those passing others signal their intentions. Well, most of the time.

You and everyone around you has proven that you know the rules by taking an exam. If you don't know the rules, you don't get a driver's license. If you don't follow the rules, you risk getting a ticket.

There are rules governing driving a boat, too. They're called the *International Regulations for Preventing Collisions at Sea*, or COLREGS. The U.S. Coast Guard publishes a booklet entitled *Navigation Rules, International–Inland.* These rules apply to all vessels navigating in U.S. waters.

The COLREGS originally came about in the 1800s with the advent of power-driven vessels. Until then, sailing ships, being relatively slow, rarely collided. After a few too many ships ran into each other, however, authorities in England, the United States, France, and about thirty other countries signed into law what have evolved over the years into our present day International Rules of the Road.

Note that the title uses the words "international." No matter where you go boating, whether it's in your home waters or while chartering a boat in the Virgin Islands, the French Riviera, or the South Pacific, the rules for avoiding collisions with other vessels are essentially the same.

That's comforting.

What's a bit disconcerting, though, is that in the United States you don't need a license to drive a boat. That's right. Anybody with a check book can buy or charter a boat and within minutes be driving around on the water without a clue as to what the rules are.

And believe me, those people are out there.

Luckily, collisions between two boats are relatively rare. Most people do know the rules, because it's foolish not to learn them.

This chapter will give you an overview of the COLREGS. By studying the information here, you'll understand how they work and what's expected of you when you operate a boat. But don't leave port without a copy of the actual regulations. These can be found online at http://www.navcen.uscg.gov/mwv/navrules/rotr_online.htm. You can buy them at any marine store and in most general bookstores. Get a copy and read them from beginning to end. Only then will you know all that's expected of you.

Be aware that there is a set of rules that applies only to inland waters of the U.S. This set of inland water rules differs in some areas from the international rules. Inland waters include rivers, bays, and harbors. But guess what? Some waters that you might think would qualify as "inland," such as Puget Sound and most waters in Maine, fall under the international rules. It can be a bit confusing. I'll cover the general rules with which you should be familiar, but you'll have to sort out whether the waters on which you'll be boating are inland or international, then consult the COLREGS yourself.

Your goal should be to know the nautical Rules of the Road as well as you know the rules for driving a car. You should be able to react immediately to any encounter with another craft, to identify vessels at night by their lights, and to know what those horn blasts you hear mean. You want to be a safe and competent mariner, and to do that, you have to know, understand, and apply these rules.

Steering and Sailing Rules

The COLREGS apply to all vessels.[5] A *vessel* is any craft that moves through the water by other than human or animal propulsion. Animal propulsion? That's right—a canal barge towed by a couple of mules is not considered a vessel. Human-propelled boats include kayaks, canoes, and rowboats. These guys don't have to follow the rules; they merely must use good common sense. The term "vessel" covers ships, powerboats, and sailboats, as well as submarines and seaplanes.

When you're on your vessel, all other vessels have to follow the same rules as you do, but there is a hierarchy of responsibility. When you encounter another vessel, you either have the right of way and are called the *stand-on vessel*, or you do not have the right of way, and are called the *give-way vessel*. Generally, the stand-on vessel maintains course and speed and the give-way vessel must get out of the stand-on vessel's way.

A vessel's ranking in the hierarchy changes depending on the circumstances. You should always know where you stand in this pecking

[5] I have italicized any words you should make sure you understand as they apply to the regulations.

order. I recommend you commit the following list of most-privileged to least-privileged vessels to memory:

- **Most privileged**=any vessel being *overtaken.* "Overtaken" means that another vessel is coming up from astern and passing. The exact angle of approach that qualifies as overtaking is "22.5 degrees abaft the beam." That's off your port or starboard quarter and aft. (See why I put the chapter on nautical terminology first?)

- **Next most privileged**=any vessel that is *restricted in ability to maneuver* or *not under command.* The former includes, but is not limited to, large ships in narrow channels, dredges, and vessels laying pipelines or mines. The latter includes a vessel dragging anchor, a vessel whose steering has broken, and sailboats becalmed by lack of wind. All of these vessels are considered under way, but they can't move around too well. Therefore, they're privileged . . . but not as privileged as a vessel being overtaken. Get it?

- **Next most privileged**=a vessel under way that is engaged in fishing by using long lines (which can be up to a mile long), trawls, nets, or other equipment that restricts its ability to maneuver. Steer clear of these guys. A *vessel engaged in fishing* under this definition is almost always a commercial vessel. It does not refer to Joe Weekender out there in his Sea Ray with a couple of rods over the side.

- **Next most privileged**=a sailing vessel. Notice that I didn't write "a sailboat." Under the Rules of the Road there's a big distinction. If you are on a sailboat and are using your motor, you are considered a "power-driven vessel" and must abide by the rules that apply to power-driven vessels. Even if your sails are raised, if your engine is in gear, then by definition you're a power-driven vessel. Ok, you ask, "What if the other boat can't tell if I have my engine on?" It doesn't matter. You know it's on, and the rules are the rules. As in all other situations covered by the COLREGS, if you are required to get out of the other vessel's way, make your move obvious enough that he can instantly tell you are giving way to him.

- **Second-to-last least privileged**=a power-driven vessel. This is your basic ship, megayacht, trawler, cigarette boat, runabout, charter fishing boat, and any other boat propelled by a motor or engine that has no restrictions on its ability to move around.

- **Least privileged vessel**=a seaplane. Look, these guys have the whole sky to fly around in, so if they want to pretend they're a boat, the Rules say they have to stay out of everybody else's way. It's only fair.

So how does this all work? Easy. Anyone higher on the list than you are will be the stand-on vessel with the right of way. Anyone lower than you is the give-way vessel and must give way to you. That means they must stay clear of you and/or maneuver to avoid collision with you. The moment you see another vessel out there on the water with you, and there is a chance you'll be maneuvering near each other, you should immediately ask yourself, "Am I the stand-on or give-way vessel?"

If you're the stand-on vessel, do not change your course. Do not increase or decrease your speed. If you're the give-way vessel, make a clear and obvious turn or increase or decrease your speed to avoid collision. Them's the rules.

Starting at the bottom of the list, you can see that seaplanes must steer clear of everyone else on the list, unless their engine dies and they are adrift. Next come power vessels. They steer clear of everyone on the list above them, except for seaplanes.

Sailing vessels (sailboats using their sails and not their engines) only have to steer clear of the vessels above them on the list, that is: vessels engaged in fishing, vessels restricted in their ability to maneuver or not under command, or any vessel that the sailboat is overtaking. This is an important distinction that many people overlook: If you are a really fast-sailing vessel and you decide to sail right past a slowpoke powerboat going the same direction as you are, you are the give-way vessel, even though you're sailing.

Why? Because once you decide to overtake someone, your position in the pecking order changes. An overtaken vessel is always the most privileged. Everyone on that list, whether sailboat or a large ship restricted in its ability to maneuver, must stay clear of a vessel they're overtaking because they then become the give-way vessel, according to the Rules of the Road.

This may all seem rather complicated. Don't let it get to you. The majority of the boats you'll encounter on the water will be power-driven vessels and sailing vessels.

Let's test your understanding. I was sailing near Annapolis, Maryland one summer and had just passed under the Chesapeake Bay Bridge. It was a beautiful day and the harbor was crowded with pleasure boats. The course I was steering took me right across the path of a small runabout. Two guys were sitting at the stern of the boat drinking beer and fishing. Who had the right of way?

I did. Why? Because I was a sailing vessel and they were under way on a power-driven vessel. Unfortunately, it quickly became obvious that they weren't going to move, and I was forced to head up into the wind to avoid a collision. I voiced my displeasure as I sailed past, only to be told in a very superior tone that they were a "fishing vessel." Obviously, they only got as far as the part of the most-privileged list that said, "vessel engaged in fishing" and stopped reading. Guys, those little rods don't qualify as lines, nets, or trawls.

This raises another important rule: You must do everything possible to avoid collision, no matter if you are the stand-on vessel or not. If the risk of collision appears imminent, you must maneuver to avoid one. So in spite of the fact that I had the right of way, as soon as it became obvious that the beer-guzzling anglers weren't going to move, it was my responsibility to do so.

Ok, now you understand the pecking order that determines who has the right of way between vessels with differing abilities to maneuver. But what about when two power-driven vessels encounter one another? Or two sailboats? There's a set or rules for each type of boat, of course, so here goes:

<u>**Power Vessels**</u>:

• Meeting: When two power vessels meet head on or nearly head on, they should each alter course to starboard and pass port to port. Don't let the "port and starboard" thing confuse you. This is just like meeting a car on a narrow road. You pass the same way unless it's dangerous to do so. It's ok to pass starboard to starboard once in a while if conditions warrant. (See Fig. 9.1, below)

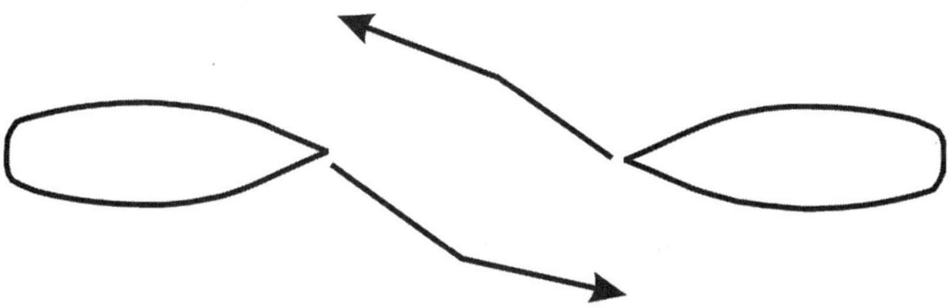

Fig. 9.1

• Crossing: When one vessel is going to cross the path of another, the one to the right has the right of way. Notice how easy that is to remember: *Right* has the *right of way*. If you're driving a power-driven vessel and you see a boat coming toward you from the right, it has the right of way and you must slow down, speed up, or turn to avoid collision. If it is to your left, then obviously you are on its right. If you're on its right, then you have the right of way. You are the stand-on vessel, so you just keep on going. You only need to maneuver if it becomes clear that the other guy doesn't know his Rules of the Road and isn't giving way. (See Fig 9.2, below.)

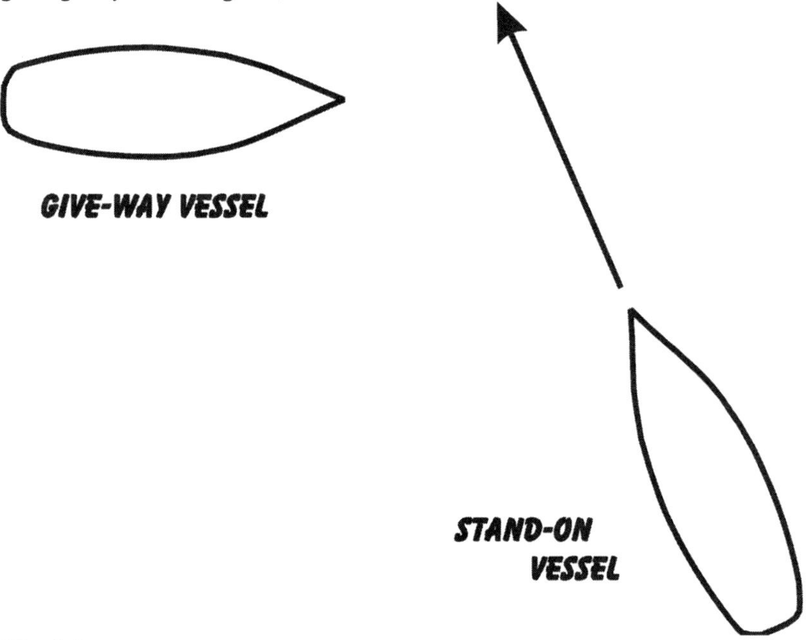

Fig. 9.2

• Overtaking: We discussed this above. If you are overtaking another vessel, you must steer clear of it. Conversely, if you notice that someone is overtaking you, you must maintain your course and speed until overtaken. In other words, you cannot suddenly turn right and cut the guy off. That would be a big no-no. (See Fig. 9.3, next page.)

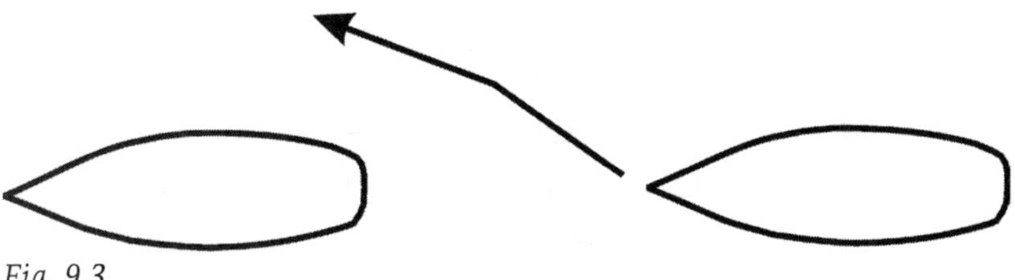

Fig. 9.3

Sailing Vessels:

(To understand these rules, you must first know that when a sailboat's sails are out on the port side because the wind is coming across the boat's starboard side, the sailboat is said to be on a "starboard tack." Conversely, when the sails are out on the starboard side because the wind is blowing across the port side, the boat is on a port tack. Ask yourself, "Which side is the wind coming from?" Port side? Port tack. Starboard side? Starboard tack.) (See Fig. 9.4, below.)

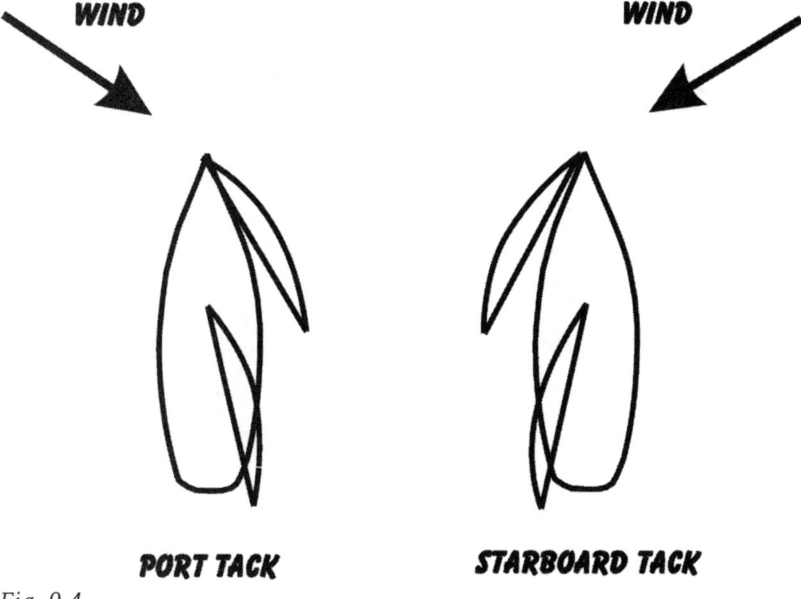

Fig. 9.4

- Meeting or Crossing:

o If both sailing vessels have the wind on the same side, the one closest to the wind is the give-way vessel (because it's easier for him to maneuver). Note in figure 9.5 (below) that the vessel to the right is the give-way vessel because he is to windward (closer to the wind). If these two boats were power vessels, or if the boat to the left were a power vessel, the boat to the right would be the stand-on vessel. This is a crucial difference, so be sure you understand it.

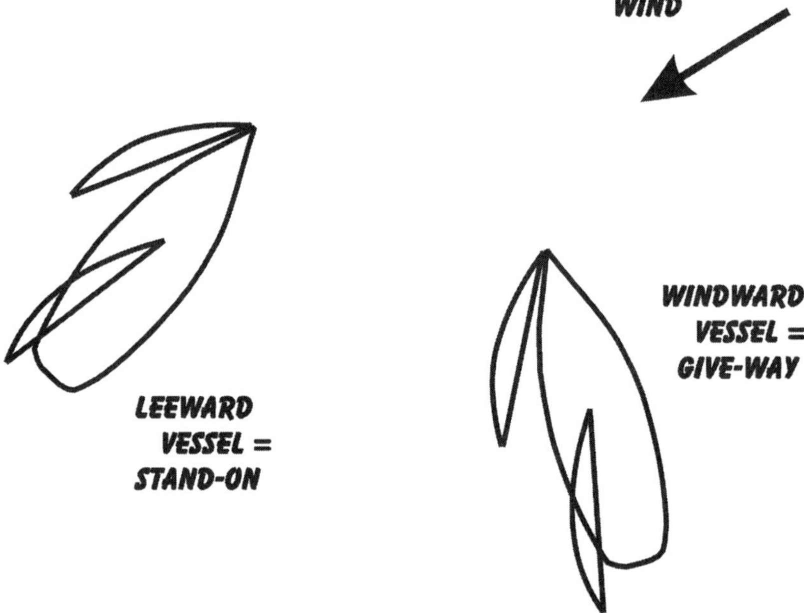

Fig. 9.5

Meeting or Crossing (continued)

o If each vessel has the wind on a different side (one is on starboard tack and the other is on port tack), the one on starboard tack has the right of way. (See Fig. 9.6 below.) This makes for another easy memory device: starboard is the same as right, so once again, starboard is right. If you're on port tack and you encounter a sailboat on starboard tack, you must give way. This is just like the situation in figure 9.5, where, unlike when two power-driven vessels cross, the vessel to the right must give way.

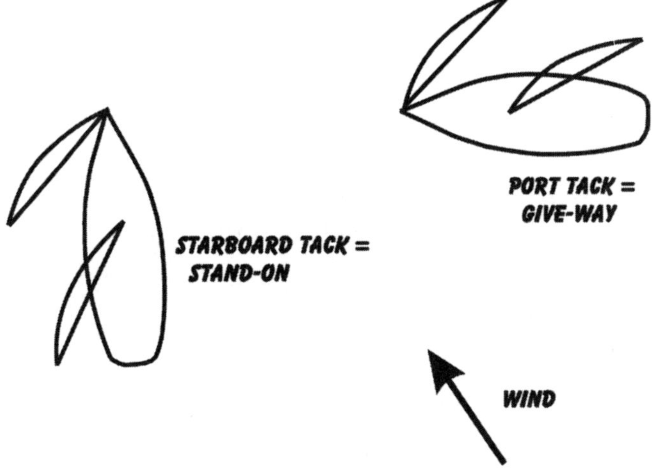

Fig. 9.6

• Overtaking: Same as any overtaking situation: the overtaken vessel stands on while the overtaking vessel is the give-way vessel and must maneuver to avoid collision.

You only need to remember these sailing rules if you are a sailor. If you're a power boater, simply remember that you must always give way to sailing vessels unless they are overtaking you.

By now I'm sure you're catching on, but how about a quiz:

> You're on a sailboat, sailing along without using your engine. You see that you're going to cross paths with a 900-foot cargo ship. You are to starboard of the ship in a crossing situation. Who has the right of way? (Tick, tock, tick, tock, tick, tock . . .)
>
> Answer: You do, according to the Rules of the Road, because: 1) you are a sailing vessel and 2) you are to the right of the power-driven vessel. Wow. Two reasons that make you the stand-on vessel.

But this is real life, not just a what-if drill. Who should really maneuver to avoid collision?

Suzanne says: you should, according to the Law of Gross Tonnage. Yes, the Rules rule, but when it comes to big ships, let common sense take precedence. You can maneuver a lot easier than they can. Why push it?

One of the funniest boating stories I ever heard came from a couple we met while cruising in the Bahamas. When they began their sailing adventure, neither had ever been sailing. The wife knew next to nothing, and the husband knew only what he'd read in books. They agreed to buy a brand new 41-foot cutter on the condition that she would be displayed at the Newport boat show. The broker told them he'd give them three days of lessons immediately following the show.

Unfortunately, the broker left town without teaching them a thing. Our friends were in a hurry to get to the islands and figured they could learn as they went. So they sailed straight out into the ocean and headed south. How hard could it be?

Well, night fell, and hubby decided to get some rest. He sat his wife at the helm, pointed out the number at the top of the compass, and told her, "Just keep the boat moving in this direction. I'll be up in a couple of hours."

So our friend was sailing merrily along in the dark, singing and smiling, no doubt, when across the horizon came an enormous ship. It was lighted up like an alien spacecraft. She picked up the VHF radio and said exactly this: "*Big Ship, Big Ship*, this is *Voyager*."[6]

The ship answered back, "*Voyager*, this is the *Ocean Princess*."

Our friend said, "*Ocean Princess*, this is *Voyager*. Could you tell me how many people you have on your bridge?"

The cruise liner replied, "*Voyager*, we have five people on our bridge at this time."

I would love to have been a fly on the wall of that bridge when she replied, "Well, there's five of you and only one of me, so will you please stay out of my way?"

Oh, my goodness.

The ship kindly agreed to maneuver around her, but everyone on the bridge no doubt was shaking their head at the clueless woman out there on the water in the dark. In the years since that incident, our friends on *Voyager* have become very competent sailors, logging thousands of miles at sea. It proves the point, however, that you must never assume that everyone out there knows the rules.

Determining if a Risk of Collision Exists

This is not actually part of the Rules of the Road, but it's a good time to discuss how to tell if you might hit that other vessel out there on the water with you. I'm always amazed how you can be on a wide

[6] Boat names have been changed to protect the guilty as well as the innocent.

expanse of water with only one other vessel and your paths will cross within feet. It's almost as if boats have a sort of magnetic attraction to each other.

When you're driving a car, things happen fast. You look up, adrenaline rushes to your heart, and you think, *Oh my gosh, that truck's going to hit me!*

It's not always quite so obvious on a boat.

The moment you notice another vessel that's under way, stare straight at him and notice what point on your boat he's lined up with. For example, say a ship appears off your starboard bow at about a 45-degree angle. When you look at it, perhaps you're looking straight through the third stanchion back from your bow pulpit.

Keep watching that ship and note how its position changes in relation to that third stanchion:

- If the ship moves to the left of the stanchion, it's going to pass ahead of you.
- If the ship moves to the right of the stanchion, it's going to pass astern of you.
- If, as the two of you continue on your respective tracks, the ship's position in relation to the stanchion remains the same (that is, the ship stays right there lined up with the third stanchion), a risk of collision definitely exists. The technical term for this situation is Constant Bearing, Decreasing Range, or CBDR. The vessel's bearing in relation to you is constant/unchanging, and its range is decreasing/it's getting closer. If you notice that you're in a CBDR situation, determine who has the right of way, and either stand on or give way accordingly. And, as always, if the other vessel fails to take appropriate action and a risk of collision exists, you must maneuver.

Lights and Shapes

This is the section of the Rules of the Road that I find the most fascinating because it's so ingenious. Like the drafters of the U.S. Constitution, the people who wrote the *International Regulations for Preventing Collisions at Sea* came up with a brilliant plan that covers all the bases, but unlike the Constitution, the COLREGS leave no room for interpretation. What you see is what you get.

If you've ever been under way on your boat at night, you know that it can be pretty dark out there. You move through the blackness with no streetlights or headlights to show you what's around. All you have are your instruments, your eyes, and your ears. It sounds a little intimidating, but actually, nighttime on the water is great. Why? Because it's so easy to identify immediately what kind of vessel you're looking at and which way it's moving.

All vessels must display lights from sunset to sunrise and during periods of restricted visibility, such as in fog. There are five basic lights that are the same for all power-driven vessels:

- A stern light: a white light that is only visible in an arc of 135 degrees centered at the stern (used only when under way).
- A masthead or "steaming" light: a white light that is only visible in an arc of 225 degrees centered at the bow (used only when under way).
- A starboard running light: a green light that is only visible from the bow of the vessel and out in a 112.5 degree arc to starboard (used only when under way).
- A port running light: a red light that is only visible from the bow of the vessel and out in a 112.5 degree arc to port (used only when under way).
- An anchor light: a single white light that is visible in an arc of 360 degrees (used only when at anchor).

Note: Sailboats under sail display the same stern light and red and green running lights as power-driven vessels, but they only use their masthead light when under power.

If you're mathematically talented, you'll immediately notice two things:

1. The arc of visibility of the port and starboard lights combined is the same as the arc of visibility of the masthead light: 225 degrees.

2. The arc of visibility of the masthead light and stern light combined is 360 degrees, or a complete circle.

This is the ingenious part. Because of their limited arcs of visibility, when you see just a red or green light out there in the darkness without a masthead light, you instantly know you are looking at a sailing vessel under way. You can tell from the color of the light which side you're looking at. For example, if you see a red light, you're looking at a sailing vessel's port side. If you move farther aft in relation to the vessel, you'll no longer see his port running light, but will see his white stern light, instead. If you see red or green with white above it, you're looking at a power-driven vessel.

Several years ago we were completing a northbound transit of the Intracoastal Waterway and emerged from the Elizabeth River after sunset into the harbor at Portsmouth, Virginia. A voice came over our radio and said, "Calling the sailboat off my port bow just past Hospital Point, this is *Symphony*." I could only see one other boat, and it was approaching us off our port bow, so I knew the guy was calling us.

I answered, "This is sailing vessel *Liberty*."

Symphony replied, "Roger, *Liberty*, I just wanted to let you know your starboard running light is burned out." I lowered the microphone and looked forward. I could clearly see the glow of both the red and green lights reflected against our bow pulpit, so I answered, "*Symphony, Liberty.* Our starboard running light is working just fine."

He replied, "No, it's not, because I can't see it from here."

I looked over at his boat. We were both viewing each other from the same angle, off our respective port bows. From my vantage point, all I could see was his port running light, just as he could only see ours. I raised the mike and replied, "*Symphony, Liberty.* You can't see our starboard running light because you're not supposed to see it from that angle."

There was a long pause, after which the man's rather testy voice remarked, "Well, I was only trying to be helpful."

Be aware, it's just as important to know all of the lights required under the rules as it is to know the steering and sailing rules.

The lights just described are required on all vessels over 7 meters—about 21 feet. Anything shorter than that must display an all-around white light. It only has to use red and green running lights if practical.

Vessels over fifty meters (about 150 feet) in length are different. Because they're so long, they must display two masthead lights—the ones that are visible in an arc of 225 degrees centered at the bow. These two lights must be placed on the ship to form a range.

Now, this is really cool. Imagine you're looking at a big ship directly head on. What will you see? You'll see both the red and green running lights and its two white masthead lights with one directly above the other. If you're both under way, this is a view that you really don't want to see, unless he's very far away. (See Figure 9.7, next page. Note that in all the following diagrams, W=white, R=red, G=green, Y=yellow.)

But what happens as you change relative position? Those two masthead lights appear to separate. I am awed every time I see huge ships at night, like this (see Figure 9.8, next page):

These mammoth vessels are reduced to nothing more than a few lights. As your position relative to a ship changes from looking directly at its bow to looking at its beam, the masthead lights get farther, and farther, and farther apart until you realize just how long the vessel really is.

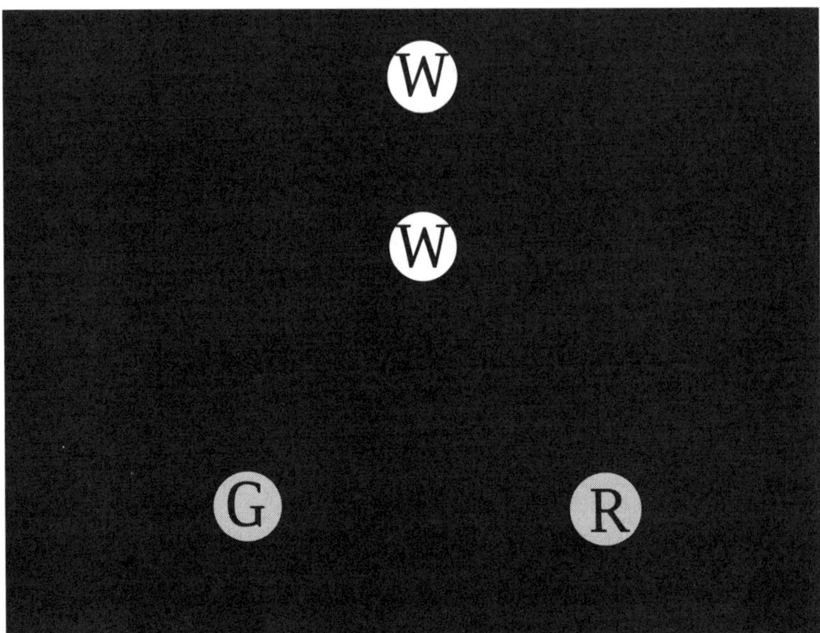

Fig. 9.7: Vessel head-on view

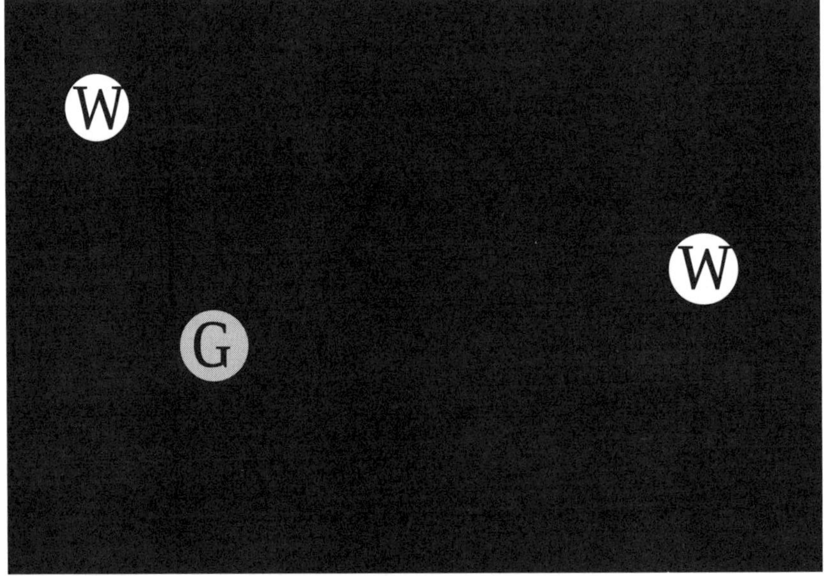

Fig. 9.8: Vessel starboard side view (over 50 meters)

If all you see is a single white light, you're either looking at an under-way vessel's stern light (from astern, obviously) or a vessel at anchor (from any angle). Big ships are even more impressive when they turn and head away from you. After the angle from which you're viewing it increases beyond the 112.5 degree arc of the running lights, all you see is a single white stern light. It's hard to believe there's fifty thousand tons of ship in front of that one bulb.

Fig. 9.9

The lights we've covered so far are for your standard power-driven and sailing vessels. But what about the other vessels out there doing special things like fishing and towing? Or those poor guys who are restricted in their ability to maneuver or who are adrift? Yes, you guessed it: they have special lights all their own.

I won't go into every set of lights. You need to review all the rules anyway, and you'll find every type of vessel in there. I will go over a few of the more common lights you're apt to see and describe how they're displayed.

• **Towing vessels**: If a tugboat is towing an object such as a barge that is 200 meters or less astern of the tug, it is required to display two white 225-degree masthead lights in a vertical line (on the same mast) in addition to red and green sidelights. If you see this tug from astern, you won't see its masthead or port and starboard running lights because they're shielded. What you will see, however, is a yellow light above the stern light. If you see any of these combinations, do not pass closely astern of the tug or you may cut between the tug and its tow. That could prove disastrous. (See Figure 9.10 below and Figure 9.11, next page.

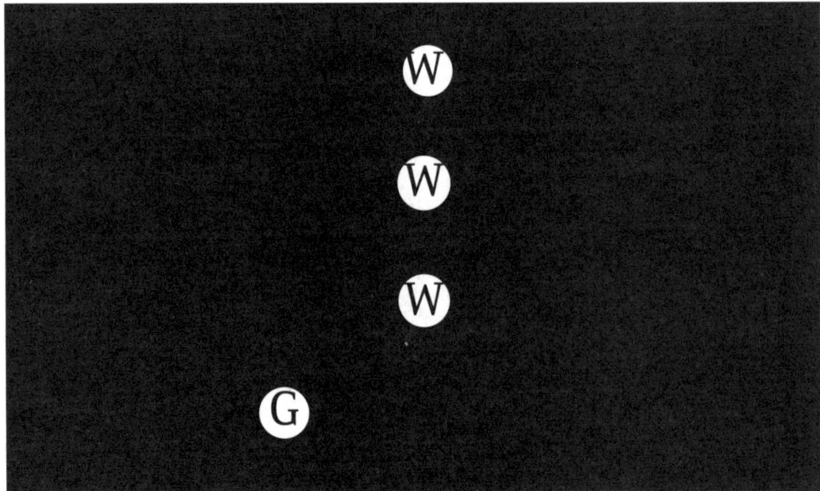

Fig. 9.10: Vessel towing astern, starboard side view (less than 50 meters)

Note 1: If the towing vessel is longer than 50 meters, it will also display an additional masthead light to form a range with the two vertical masthead lights.

Note 2: The barge should also display red and green sidelights as well as a stern light. These lights may be very dim, because they are usually lighted by small batteries or may even be small kerosene lamps. The lights on the tug itself are always much brighter.

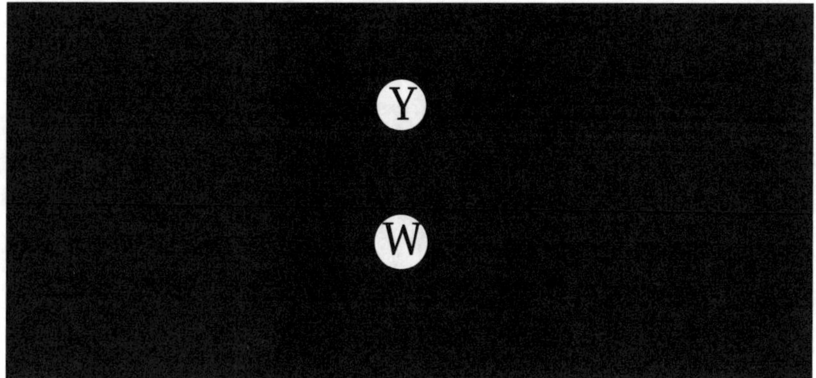

Fig. 9.11: Vessel towing astern, seen from astern

What if the barge is more than 200 meters astern of the tug? In that case, the tug will display three white masthead lights in a vertical line, in addition to all the other lights mentioned above.

- **Vessels engaged in fishing** (with lines, trawls, nets, etc.) display an all-around/360 degree red light over an all-around/360 degree white light. If it is under way, such a vessel will also display the standard running lights and stern light. (See Figure 9.12, next page.)

There are mnemonic devices to make it easier to remember most of these special situations. Examples include: "Red over white, fishing at night" and "White over red, pilot ahead." Study them all and make flashcards of the various scenarios, if that helps. See how many you can guess before you get out on the water, then put your skills to the test.

Each of the special lights has a corresponding shape that must be displayed between sunrise and sunset. You'll usually only see these on commercial ships or naval vessels. All shapes are black and consist of balls, diamonds, cones, cylinders, and combinations of these.

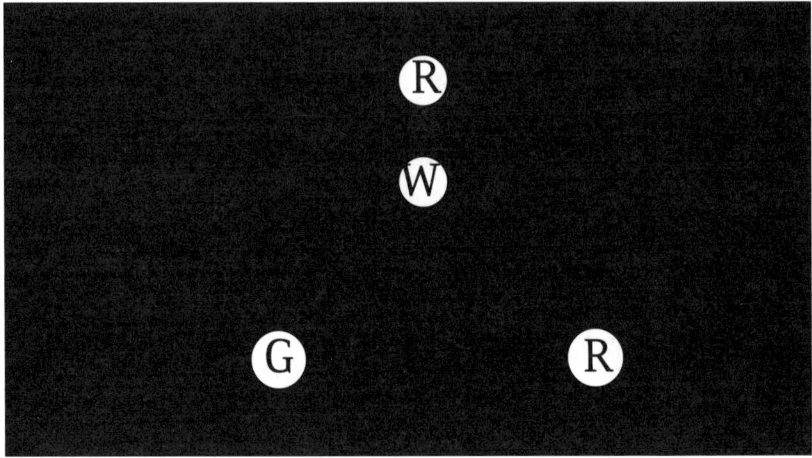

Fig. 9.12: Vessel engaged in fishing, head-on view

The most common one you're likely to see is a single black ball on a vessel at anchor. This is very helpful when you spot a ship in the distance and can't see if his anchor is down or not. If there's a black ball hanging over his deck near the bow, then he's at anchor and no risk of collision exists.

Sound and Light Signals

The Rules include a series of sound signals with corresponding flashing light signals to convey a variety of messages. The word "whistle" refers to a sound-producing device, whether it's a whistle or a horn. You'll hear plenty of commercial vessels making the following signals, but only a handful of recreational boaters comply. Note that a prolonged blast should last from four to six seconds. A short blast lasts one second.

Here are the more common sound signals. Please consult the actual COLREGS to review them all:

- 5 short blasts: the danger/doubt signal. This is sounded when a vessel doesn't understand the actions or intentions of another vessel within sight of it, or when the other vessel doesn't appear to be taking sufficient action to avoid collision. The most common scenario I've seen is a large ship leaving a harbor and a small recreational boater lollygagging about in the channel, oblivious to the mammoth bearing down on him. You don't hear five blasts too often, but when you do, it's an attention-grabber.

- 3 short blasts: sounded by a vessel to indicate "I am operating astern propulsion." This is the nautical equivalent of that little beep-beep-beep sound that delivery trucks and forklifts make when they're backing up.
- 1 prolonged blast: indicates a vessel is getting under way from a dock or berth, under the inland rules, or approaching a blind bend, under international and inland rules.

Power vessels, mostly commercial boats, give maneuvering signals when they meet or overtake other vessels in narrow channels. The different signals and the required responses are listed in the COLREGS. I've heard recreational boaters use these signals while cruising up and down the Intracoastal Waterway, but most will simply call on the VHF and discuss how they'd like to pass.

Sometimes commercial vessel operators will verbalize their intentions by referring to sound signals instead of actually blowing a whistle. A tugboat captain may call you on the radio and test your knowledge by saying, "I'll pass you on one whistle." That means he is going to alter course to starboard and pass you port side to port side. A "two-whistle pass" means the vessel will alter course to port and pass you starboard to starboard. (A good way to remember these is that "port" has one syllable, so a one-whistle pass means "pass port to port." "Starboard" has two syllables, so a two-whistle pass means, "pass starboard to starboard."

As a recreational boater, you may never use the sound signals above, but you should recognize them when you hear them. There is a set of sound signals which you should know and use, however: fog signals. You can go out on a perfectly clear day and within an hour not be able to see fifty feet. You can't count on the other guys out there having radar, so you want them to be able to hear you coming; you also want to be able to recognize who they are.

When we cruised the coast of Maine for the first time, we were relative novices at the fog game. At first we blew our fog signals with a little plastic horn that emitted a pitiful bleat that would only have been heard by someone in a kayak ten feet away. The lobstermen out there motoring back and forth would never have heard us over their engines. We moved up to one of those air horns that fans blow at football games, but with all the fog we encountered, those quickly ran out of juice.

At $20 apiece, we realized we'd go broke blowing fog signals with the compressed air horns because we were continuing to more remote areas where we'd be unable to resupply. So Ty decided to improve our capabilities.

We went to an auto parts store, where he bought a car horn, a fuse, a toggle switch, and a cigarette lighter adaptor. He mounted the horn on a stick, wired it all up, and plugged it into the 12-volt outlet by our helm. By using the toggle switch, we were able to blow the horn in the appropriate signal for either a sailing vessel or a power-driven vessel, whichever we happened to be at the time. It worked great. The only problem was, other vessels who heard it thought there was a '57 Chevy in the harbor.

For your purposes, the compressed air horns will do just fine. Here are the signals with which you should be familiar:

- One prolonged blast at least every two minutes: power-driven vessel under way. This applies to big ships as well as little runabouts.

Note: if a vessel is dead in the water—technically called under way but not making way (such as a vessel that is drifting while fishing)—it must sound two prolonged blasts.

• One prolonged blast followed by three short blasts at least every two minutes: a manned vessel being towed.

• One prolonged blast followed by two short blasts at least every two minutes: just about everyone else. This includes sailing vessels, vessels constrained by draft (those which draw so much water that they can't maneuver easily), vessels restricted in their ability to maneuver, vessels engaged in fishing, and vessels towing or pushing.

Putting this into context, when we sail in fog without the engine, we blow one prolonged blast followed by two short blasts (whommmmmmmmmmmm, whom, whom). If we have the engine in gear, we blow one prolonged blast. Note that if you find yourself in fog and need to use sound signals, be sure to warn your partner before blowing the horn.

There are additional sound signals for vessels at anchor or aground, and the Rules even include the requirement for vessels over 100 meters to ring bells. I doubt you'll ever have to ring a bell, but see the COLREGS for details.

Phew. This is a lot to remember, isn't it? And there's more, such as the requirement to maintain a proper lookout at all times, even if the lookout is the helmsman. Yes, you can duck below to use the head or get a soda, but if you were to collide with another vessel, you would be at fault for not maintaining a proper lookout.

Make sure the lookout knows that he or she is the lookout. If the boat's on autopilot or something happens to sidetrack you, like losing a hat overboard, it's easy for everyone aboard to get distracted. Specifically assign someone to keep an eye on things while you're taking care of whatever it is that has interrupted normal maneuvers. Maintain situational awareness at all times, before something sneaks up and bites you.

As I mentioned at the beginning of this chapter, you don't need to pass a test to operate a boat—a recreational boat, that is. If you want to earn money running a vessel, whether it's by operating a charter boat or teaching sailing lessons, in the U.S. you need a Captain's license, issued by the U.S. Coast Guard. To earn such a license, you must fulfill time on the water requirements, pass a drug test, provide letters of recommendation, and pass an exam.

The test is rigorous, spread out over two days and broken down into various areas of expertise. Prospective captains have to earn a grade of 70 percent to pass the exam, with one major exception: the Rules of the Road require a minimum passing score of 90 percent. Earn less than an "A" on the collision regulations, and the test-taker fails the entire exam.

I'd say the Coast Guard recognizes the importance of knowing the rules.

And so should you. When it comes to the COLREGS, aim to be an "A" student. I want to stress again that I have not covered all the rules here. This has been an overview to get you started and give you a basic understanding of how they work. Pick up a copy of the Rules of the Road and prepare for your next test.

The real one.

10

Navigation & Piloting

Allow me to introduce Stella. She's embarking on an adventure. She's going to go hiking in the desert north of Las Vegas. She hit it big with the slots, so she invested some of her winnings in all the latest camping gear and a pair of sturdy boots. She drives about twenty miles outside the city and leaves her car along the roadside. She sets off and heads toward the hills. There are no paths out here, but that's kind of neat. She's free to go wherever she pleases.

Stella hikes for hours through culverts and past colorful rock formations, taking lots of pictures with her new digital camera. Her car is long out of sight when she sets up camp. In spite of that annoying coyote howling from that hill over yonder, she enjoys a beautiful night sleeping under the stars.

The next morning, it's time to head back to her nice comfy hotel. Stella packs up her tent and erases all signs of her visit. She hikes about a hundred yards, then stops. Everything kind of looks the same out here. She scratches her head. Umm. Which way, exactly, is the car?

This could be a problem.

Stella starts to panic, then remembers the GPS. The little handheld Global Positioning System they sold her at the outdoor shop is the latest model. It has all the bells and whistles and will tell her exactly where she is. She turns it on and this is what she sees: N 36°59.258' W 115°15.867'.

And that's supposed to mean something? Stella thinks.

Hmmm. Maybe she should have read the manual. The one that's back in the car. No problem. Stella digs through her backpack and pulls out the map the salesman recommended she take along. She spreads it out on the red dirt and stares down at it. She squints, then frowns. It's nothing but a bunch of concentric circles. What are all those numbers inside the circles? And why is everything green? Where are the red and blue lines she's used to?

Yep, you guessed it. Stella's in trouble. You know what's going to happen when she turns on her cell phone: "No service." Perhaps she should have taken a lesson in land navigation before setting out. And maybe learned how to read a topographic map? And possibly figured out how to use the data her GPS provides?

It's unthinkable that anyone would set out across a desert without these skills. That would be like somebody getting under way in a boat without knowing how to read a chart or use a GPS.

As if.

When I was preparing to retire from the Navy to go cruising full time, one of my sailors, a desk-bound yeoman who had never been to sea, asked me how I'd be able to know where I was going. Her question caught me off guard. With my charts, of course. She couldn't grasp the concept that you could be out on the open water with no roads or signs, and still figure out how to get from point A to point B.

Thanks to my yeoman, I'm not going to assume anything. I'm going to give you the basics of navigation here—the bare minimum you need to understand when you leave port in your boat. If you already know this stuff, good on you. If not, make sure you understand it, then continue to hone your skills. You may still run aground some day, especially if you visit Chesapeake Bay (they say that there are two types of boaters on the Chesapeake . . . those who have gone aground, and those who will go aground), but at least you'll be able to look at your nautical chart and figure out how you made such a mistake.

So what exactly is navigation? It's the method of safely guiding a vessel from one place to another. You may see books dealing with "navigation and piloting." Piloting is the type of navigation where you use reference points around you to locate your position, as opposed to finding your way in open water. Reference points include coastal landmarks and navigation aids, such as buoys and daymarks, water depths, and so forth. Pilot waters, therefore, are coastal areas, bays, sounds, rivers, and lakes.

The advent of the Global Positioning System has revolutionized recreational boating. No longer do boaters have to steer by the stars. Thanks to a network of satellites that provide positioning data straight into commercially available receivers—your GPS unit—boaters now need only push a button to know their position with an accuracy previously unheard of.

Unfortunately, it's all too easy to plug a GPS into a laptop computer loaded with navigational software, or to turn on a chart plotter to find out where you are. Rather than learning how to navigate properly, many boaters rely on these modern electronic gadgets to guide them. But what happens if your unit dies? Or the GPS system crashes? Or what if the information on your navigation software is incorrect? There have been times when our computer screen has shown the symbol representing our boat traveling right over land, when we were clearly on the water. Had we been relying solely on the software in the fog, we would have been in serious trouble.

I strongly recommend that if you use a chart plotter or computer-based navigation software aboard your boat, you use it only as a backup to paper charts. If that's asking too much, then at least ensure you have the paper charts or chart books on board and know how to read and use them.

The best way to learn to navigate, in my opinion, is to take a course or have a tutor. You can learn a lot from books, to be sure, but you'll need to learn to use some special navigation tools. Kindergarten skills may apply for things like drawing lines and circles, but unless you are a draftsman, using parallel rulers and dividers may present a totally new challenge. I recommend that somebody show you how they work. Check your local Power Squadron or Coast Guard Auxiliary for a schedule of classes, or find a sailing or boating school.

In the meantime, let me give you a taste of how all this navigating works.

If you have a navigational chart available (and please, never call it a map), I recommend you open it while reading this section. The first thing you'll notice is the color coding. Water is generally blue or white, but it can be light green or yellow in shoaling areas. Note that there's a lot of writing on your chart—not just the names of places, but sometimes entire paragraphs. Many of these are cautionary notes that you should read before you use the chart.

See those numbers superimposed on the water? Those are called soundings. They indicate the depth of the water at that particular spot. The first thing you should do whenever you look at a chart is determine what type of measurements the soundings represent. In a corner of the chart you will find one of the following phrases in large letters: "Soundings in Feet" or "Soundings in Meters" or "Soundings in Fathoms." One meter equals 3.3 feet and one fathom equals 6 feet.

Suppose you're under way in your boat and you're heading for a cove where the soundings show a mixture of 1s and 2s. Your boat draws 6 feet, so you want at least 7 feet of water under you, preferably more. Unless you've first checked the chart to determine if the soundings are in fathoms, meters, or feet, how will you know if you have enough water? Those 1s and 2s could represent areas of one and two feet, or 3.3 and 6.6 feet, if the soundings are in meters, or as much as 6 and 12 feet, if the soundings are in fathoms. Chart soundings in the same chart kit can change from feet to fathoms or from meters to feet from one page to the next, so always check.

The number shown is how deep the water is at Mean Lower Low Water. MLLW is the average of the lower of the two low tides each day. Be aware that the depth can go lower than that shown, but it usually doesn't. The depth indicated on your boat's depth sounder may read higher than what's on the chart, depending on the level of the tide at the time you're in that spot. For example, if the MLLW sounding, or depth, for the spot you're in is four feet, but the height of tide at the moment is six feet, your depth sounder will indicate around ten feet.

This is a good place to bring up the subject of tides. You can see why it's important to check the tides and your chart before anchoring somewhere. If you anchor based only on your depth sounder, you might be high and dry when the tide changes.

The moon exerts a gravitational pull on the earth, which affects the flow of bodies of water. This varies with the phases of the moon. In most of the United States the tide floods, then ebbs, then floods and ebbs again each day. This means there's a lot of water flowing back and forth to and from the sea. As a boater, it's critical to know how to read a tide table, since tides affect not just water depth, but currents—the speed at which the water will be moving with or against you.

At first, tide tables look like a bunch of confusing numbers, but those numbers are important. They tell you the time of each high and low tide on any given day, as well as the height of those tides. The tide is flooding when the flow of tide is going from low to high. Remember it this way: Flood=Filling in from the sea. The tide is ebbing when it goes from high to low. Remember Ebb=Emptying out to sea.

Getting back to our chart, mixed among the numbers indicating water depths are letters. These are abbreviations that represent the type of bottom in that area. For example, S indicates sand, m is for mud, and rky indicates a rocky bottom. All of these abbreviations can be found in a booklet called *Chart No. 1*. You should have a copy of *Chart No. 1* for your studies and keep it on your boat. It's not actually a chart, but a thin reference book explaining every symbol, abbreviation, shape, and object you'll see on a nautical chart.

Piloting can be fairly easy when you know where you are to start with. Charts show the shape of the landmasses around you as well as landmarks ashore, like lighthouses, church steeples, and towers. You can judge your location and follow your progress simply by checking where you are in relation to known objects. When you pass close by an object that you can identify with certainty, note your position on the chart by penciling in a small circle with a dot in the center. Write the time on a horizontal slant next to the circle. Congratulations . . . you've just plotted a fix.

Recreational boaters in the United States are lucky. Thanks to the U.S. Coast Guard, we have navigation aids throughout our waters that are well-maintained and highly reliable. This is not the case in places like the Bahamas, where you're lucky if a shallow area, or shoal, is marked with a crooked stick.

Navigation aids include buoys (both lighted and unlighted), daymarks, lighthouses, and range markers. Buoys and daymarks are color-coded and numbered. Lights can be red, green, yellow, or white, and can flash in a variety of patterns. All of these differences exist to distinguish one navigation aid from the other. You'll rarely find two lights with the same pattern or two buoys with the same number near one another.

Once you've identified that you're looking at, say, green daymark number two, and you know more or less where you are on your chart, you can easily pinpoint your position by finding green daymark number two on your chart. Note that green daymarks are always odd-numbered, while red daymarks are even.

There are specific chart symbols for each type of navigation aid. These are also described in *Chart No. 1*. Study them and understand how they're used. You'll learn to trust them to guide you around dangers and to keep you in water deep enough for your boat. There's a reason one of the first things a boater learns is "red right returning" . . . .

A couple of summers ago we were sailing south on Somes Sound near Southwest Harbor, Maine. I was following the track set into our GPS, but I wasn't being especially careful about staying right on course. Ok, I admit it, I was lollygagging. It was just so beautiful, surrounded by mountains coming right down to the water and dozens of gorgeous, classic boats.

I lazily glanced off my starboard bow and noticed a red buoy. It took a moment, but something flipped a switch in my brain. Red buoy . . . I was heading toward sea . . . "Red right returning" means keep the red buoys to starboard when returning to port, not when heading to sea . . . Yikes!

I turned the wheel hard to starboard and got the red buoy on my port side as quickly as possible. As soon as I was back on the proper side of the channel marker, I looked down at the chart. I had come frighteningly close to running the boat aground. And Maine, with its rocky coastline, is one place you don't want to run aground.

Sensing the boat's sudden motion, my husband called up from below, "Everything ok up there?"

"Everything's just fine," I sang out as I caught my breath and admonished myself for breaking one of the most basic rules of piloting.

I was lucky that situation turned out ok. Navigation aids are put where they are for a reason. Aim to know them so well that your reactions when you see them become instinctual.

But how do you determine your exact location if there are no navigation aids? With your GPS. Sure, it's the easy way out, but if the system works and it makes boating safer, then by gosh, we might as well use it. Believe me, if you ever try your hand at celestial navigation, you'll appreciate the ease of GPS more than you can imagine.

Take a GPS unit with you whenever you get under way. In fact, take two, and make sure you have extra batteries. The newer models are pretty snazzy, with all kinds of capabilities. Spend an hour going through all the pages and pushing all the buttons. If there's something you don't understand, study the manual until it's clear. As a bare minimum, know how the readout on your GPS relates to the grid of lines that's superimposed on your chart.

Let me explain.

The lines running east and west on your chart are lines of latitude. Those running north and south are lines of longitude. Longitude lines are also called meridians. These are imaginary lines superimposed on the earth's surface. Anywhere in the world that you find yourself, there are invisible intersecting lines of latitude and longitude. This intersection, given in degrees of latitude and degrees of longitude, is your position. That's why you'll sometimes hear a boat's position referred to as its lat-long.

Go back to high school math and picture an x-y chart. You had to find a spot on the chart by going a certain distance along axis x and then finding where that spot intersected with axis y. It's the same with plotting your lat-long.

Look at a globe and you'll see the lines of longitude evenly spaced to the right and left, or east and west of a spot in Greenwich, England. The line of longitude known as the Prime Meridian runs straight through Greenwich, and is designated 0 degrees. Because the earth is round, a complete circle around the planet in either direction encompasses 360 degrees of longitude. For navigational purposes, we number the lines of longitude in 180 one-degree increments to the east and 180 one-degree increments to the west.

If you're in Greenwich, England, or anywhere directly north or south of there, all the way to the poles your longitude would be 0°. If you're exactly halfway around the world from Greenwich, your longitude would be 180°.

Let's say you're on the east coast of the United States, perhaps in Charleston, South Carolina. If you were, and you turned on your GPS, you'd see a number that read about W079°. That means that you are in a spot on a circle approximately 79° west of Greenwich.

Latitude works the same way, only lines of latitude run 90° north and south starting at the Equator, which is the 0° "starting point." Sitting on a boat in Charleston harbor, you are approximately 33° degrees along an arc heading north of the equator. Can you see that the North Pole would be 90° north of the Equator? So at 33 degrees north latitude, you are just over one third of the way between the Equator and the North Pole.

In Charleston, you are 79° west of Greenwich (your longitude) and 33° north of the Equator (your latitude). Therefore, your lat-long, or your position, is 33° N, 079° W. That's what those numbers on your GPS are telling you. The digits in the tenths and hundredths that follow simply fine-tune your position down to smaller increments of a degree, referred to as minutes, and hundredths of minutes. Minutes are indicated with an apostrophe (').

Note that there are 60 minutes in one degree of latitude and longitude. Beware: this has nothing whatsoever to do with a measurement of time. This is simply an angle measurement that is smaller than a full degree. Call it a "unit," a "blip," a "whozifrazz" in your mind if that helps you to see that "minutes" is simply a word that refers to 1/60th of a degree.

The cool thing is that one minute of latitude is equal in distance to one nautical mile—about 6000 feet or 2000 yards. If you travel one nautical mile with your boat, you've covered one minute of latitude. If you travel sixty miles, you've gone a full degree. Pretty neat, huh? Any time you look at a chart or a map and want to judge how far apart two places are, simply look at the latitude scale on the left or right side. Use this scale to measure the distance between the two points you've chosen. One degree of latitude=60 miles. Don't try this with longitude; it's not the same.

If you fine-tune your knowledge of the information above, you'll soon be able to use your GPS to plot your exact position on a chart. Now those numbers will mean something. Should you ever have to call the Coast Guard or a towboat, you can then read them your position as well as describe where you are verbally. Here's an example of how you would read aloud a given lat-long of 33° 46.259' N, 079° 38.154' W:

"My position is thirty-three degrees, forty-six point two five nine minutes north; zero seven nine degrees, thirty-eight point one five four minutes west. I am one mile west of red buoy number three."

Those hundredths of a minute that follow the word "point" narrow down your position to within sixty feet. If you're not interested in that kind of accuracy, you can eliminate the hundredths and simply say, "My position is thirty-three degrees, forty-six minutes north; zero seven nine degrees, thirty-eight minutes west." It's far easier to simply read degrees and minutes, without the hundredths. If someone's trying to find you, they'll still come within one mile of your location.

Once you know your position on a chart, you can figure out what direction you need to steer to get to another spot. As far as things to know on your boat, this is one of those don't-leave-home-without-it skills. You simply draw a line from your known position to the point where you want to go. Every chart has at least one compass rose drawn on it. (That's the little circle with North, South, East, West, and every point in between). Using a pair of parallel rulers, "walk" the line you drew until it overlays the compass on your chart. Where it crosses the compass rose is the course to steer to get to the point you've chosen. Turn your boat in the direction of your course and head thataway. Continue to plot your position to make sure you're on track.

As you can see, just like learning the Rules of the Road, there's a lot involved here. Entire books are dedicated to this subject.

What are the basic things you need to know to get by?

• As explained above, know how to read a chart. It's different than a road map. Charts provide so much good information that there's a whole book just to explain all the symbols: *Chart No. 1*. Get a copy.

• Understand latitude and longitude. Be able to plot your position on a chart given your lat-long from a GPS. Know how to figure out what your lat-long is without using your GPS by comparing obout what your lat-long is without using your GPS by comparing objects around you with those on your chart.

• Know how to use the following navigational tools: fixed compass, hand-bearing compass, dividers, and parallel rulers.

• Know how to use your compass to determine the bearing to another object.

• Be able to figure out the course to steer to get from where you are to where you want to go.

• Understand the difference between True and Magnetic compass headings.

• Familiarize yourself with all the screens on your GPS.

• Learn how your boat's instruments help you to navigate:

o Watch how your depth sounder coincides with the numbers on the chart.
o Understand how to steer a compass course.
o Use your boat speed indicator and the latitude scale on your chart to determine how long it will take to get from one point to another.
o Know how to use your chart plotter, but don't depend on it to the exclusion of paper charts.

• Be able to identify all the different aids to navigation. Know how they're used and what they indicate.

• Know how to find the time and height of the next high and low tides.

• If you have radar onboard, learn how to use it. Your radar can become your best friend if you have to navigate in the fog. It will help you locate the navigation aids and landmasses you see on your chart (not to mention that it will let you know if anyone's out there on the water with you).

Yes, there's a lot involved in navigating a boat, but it can be challenging and enjoyable. When you compare the information I've given you in this chapter with a textbook on navigation, I've barely scratched the surface. My goal here is to take the mystery out of something that someone else may have always done on your boat and to encourage you to at least learn the basics.

Being the boat's navigator is neither a traditionally blue nor pink job. If you find this topic really interesting, go beyond the fundamentals and take on the role for yourself.

No matter how involved you choose to get in finding your way on the water, promise me you'll never replicate a conversation like the one I overheard on our VHF radio while sailing off Norfolk, Virginia:

Voice: "Coast Guard, Coast Guard, this is *Clueless*." [7]

USCG: "*Clueless*, this is Coast Guard Group Hampton. What is the nature of your distress?"

Clueless: "Um, I'm aground."

USCG: "*Clueless*, Group Hampton. Where exactly are you, sir?"

Clueless: "I'm somewhere off Lynnhaven, inside the inlet."

USCG: "*Clueless*, Group Hampton. Stand by."

(Then a deeper, more mature voice came on the radio)

USCG: "*Clueless*, this is Group Hampton Roads. Exactly how many times in the past five days have you been aground?"

If the Coast Guard ever has to ask you this question, please sell your boat.

The next day we heard *Clueless* hailing a passing trawler on the radio. He asked if he could follow the boat down the Intracoastal Waterway because his charts were rather "inadequate." It seems he'd been

---

[7] Once again, I changed the boat's name, as I will with all those that follow.

using a Virginia road map to find his way through Hampton Roads. No wonder the guy repeatedly ran aground.

Don't be *Clueless*. Always ensure you have the proper chart for the area in which you're traveling. Know how to read it and know how to pinpoint your position on it. Road maps won't do the trick. Yes, the blue parts show where the water is, but just about everything else you need to safely navigate your boat will be missing.

You wouldn't go hiking in the desert without being able to find your way home. Don't leave the pier without the navigation basics.

11

Communications

It was a perfect night to be under way on the Mediterranean. We were doing an overnighter from the east coast of Spain to Ibiza in the Balearic Islands. I had the watch. The moon was nearly full, casting a swath of sparkling light on the water. The stars filled the sky as if someone had scattered a handful of diamonds across a black tablecloth. *Liberty* ghosted along on calm seas with her sails filled. The air was warm. I sat at the helm, keeping an eye out for other vessels and listening to the sound of oinks, snorts, and whinnies.

Yes, my VHF radio was alive. Fishing must have been slow that night, because every *pescadero* within range was entertaining himself by making obnoxious barnyard noises, blowing wolf whistles, and tapping his fingers on channel 16. It went on for hours.

Mariners are required to monitor channel 16 when under way, so I couldn't legally turn it off. I fought the urge to lower myself to their level and scream at them from my mike. Luckily, somebody did it for me, yelling, "When I find you guys, I'm going to kill you. I swear I'll kill you all!"

This was followed by an immediate chorus of cackles, grunts, and moos. Just as well I kept my mouth shut.

It was at that precise moment I realized I wasn't in Kansas anymore. You see, boaters in the United States are very good about radio discipline. Believe me, at the first sound of an oink or a moo on American VHF airwaves, a squared-away and somewhat terse voice would break in and announce, "Channel 16 is a hailing and distress channel only. Shift your traffic to a working channel. Coast Guard, out."

Sometimes it's good that Big Brother is listening.

When you do hear chatter on channel 16, it's usually because the two parties have forgotten to change channels after greeting one another. It won't be long before someone will break in and let them know. Otherwise, boaters keep channel 16 clear. They use it to hail another vessel, then quickly get off in case someone needs the channel for an emergency.

Do not get under way on your boat again unless you know how to use your VHF radio. Yes, you could make a distress call from your cell phone if in a bind, but who wants to rely on having a good signal when you need one?

A marine radio is user-friendly. You turn it on, dial the channel you want, hold the microphone in your hand, and press the button to talk. What could be easier? It's hardly more difficult than talking on the phone, which we gals do very well. So why is it that many women leave VHF communications to their husbands? Or when they do talk on the radio, they lack confidence and speak haltingly?

Could it be the knowledge that others might be listening? Well, they are, no doubt about it. The party line is alive and well on your VHF radio.

I had a medical emergency while off the coast of Newfoundland and we used our radio to call for assistance. The Canadian Coast Guard asked me switch to channel 28, then patched me through to a doctor in St. Johns. I described my somewhat personal symptoms to him over the VHF, knowing that anyone who'd been listening to our original transmission on channel 16 had likely switched channels with us to eavesdrop.

Several days later we pulled into a tiny fishing village. We joined the locals at a gathering where I was invited to dance. I declined, explaining that I was recovering from an abdominal ailment. "Oh, you're the one," the Newfie said. "We all heard ya on the radio and was real worried."

Suspicions confirmed.

Yes, like E.F. Hutton, people will listen when you talk. But a VHF radio is not just a way to hail your friends on another boat and say hi; it's also a piece of safety gear. It's your link with help should you need it. It allows you to contact other vessels if uncertain about their intentions. When you learn proper radio etiquette and terminology, there's no reason to hand the mike over to your partner. Use your radio as it's intended and speak with confidence, no matter who may overhear you.

Your radio has a number of channels that are reserved for specific reasons:

- 16: International hailing, distress, and safety
- 9: General hailing and radio checks
- 13: Inter-ship navigation safety and bridge-to-bridge communication between commercial vessels. If you try to hail a ship or tugboat on channel 16 and they don't reply, try 13.
- 22A: Used by the Coast Guard for maritime safety information and communicating with vessels during non-emergencies.
- 68: General recreational boat use. Often used by marinas.

Your radio also has specific weather channels starting with WX1, WX2, etc. that are accessed by pressing the WX button on your VHF. In the United States, these provide a continuous broadcast of current and future weather. For obvious reasons, you can't transmit on these channels.

Hailing Another Station

Even though the Coast Guard recommends you hail other vessels on channel 9, most vessels are monitoring 16, not 9. So use 16 if you must, but switch to another channel as quickly as possible.

First, state twice the name of the vessel you are calling, followed by your vessel's name stated one or two times. Some people give their name three times, but this is unnecessary and a bit excessive. As soon as the other party responds, unless it's an emergency, agree upon a station to switch to. It's a good idea to check to see what channels are clear before you initiate your call. The other vessel should acknowledge that you are switching and repeat the channel number so you know that they heard you correctly.

End each transmission except your final one with the word, "over." It's okay if you don't say it every single time, but it lets the other station know you've finished speaking and it's their turn. At the end of your conversation, terminate your radio call with the single word, "out." Do not say, "Over and out." The latter is a phrase that probably originated with Joe Friday on Dragnet. It's definitely a TV and movie thing, because it sure isn't proper radio terminology. If you want to sound as if you know what you're doing on a VHF radio, end your transmission simply with "out."

Here's how a standard radio call would go:

"*Racer, Racer*, this is *Slowpoke, Slowpoke,* over."

"*Slowpoke*, this is *Racer*."

"*Racer*, this is *Slowpoke*. Switch to (channel) 18, over."

"Switching to one-eight."

(Both parties switch to channel 18. The vessel that initiated the call should come back first.)

"*Racer*, this is *Slowpoke*, over."

"*Slowpoke*, this is *Racer.*"

"*Racer*, I'm heading in now. See you back at the marina, over."

"Roger that, I'm right behind you, over."

"Roger. This is *Slowpoke*, shifting back to 16, out."

"This is *Racer*, back to one-six, out."

Nothing to it. Remember that the VHF is not a CB or police radio. Don't call anyone "Good Buddy" or ask them, "What's your twenty?" Keep your conversations short and to the point and you'll sound like an old pro.

Radio Checks

If there's a VHF radio on your vessel, you're required to have it turned on and tuned to channel 16 while under way. While not everyone adheres to the rules, it's comforting to know that if you make a call, there should be somebody who hears you.

It's a good idea to check that your radio is transmitting and receiving well each time you go out. Technically, you should conduct radio checks on channel 9. You'll hear others do them on 16, but it's not good practice. To check your radio, turn to channel 9 and say: "Any station, any station, this is (sailing/motor) vessel *Holiday* for a radio check, over."

And that's all you need to say. Someone should answer back shortly with something like, "Read you loud and clear at Cherry Point." Simply answer, "This is *Holiday*. Roger, thank you. Out."

Crisp, clear, and to the point.

Other than calling your boating buddies to chat about what anchorage you want to choose that night, there are a number of times when it's quite handy to have and use a VHF radio:

• Calling Marinas. Most marinas generally monitor channel 16 as well as a specific channel they've chosen. This channel, usually 9 or 68, will be listed in local cruising guides. If not, hail the marina on 16 and they'll tell you what their working channel is. Be sure to acknowledge that you heard them and are switching to that channel before doing so by saying, "Roger; shifting to channel 68." You might call your regular marina to request help with docking in your slip. If visiting a different marina, you could call on the VHF to request a slip assignment.

• Hailing Bridge Operators. Low bridges that open are manned by a live person. Most bridge operators monitor channel 9, so you should hail them on 9 from the start, rather than 16. Before calling, look at your chart to determine the name of the bridge. Believe it or not, we've encountered some operators who were so picky that they wouldn't respond until we got the name of the bridge just right. A typical bridge opening request goes like this:

"Alligator River Bridge, Alligator River Bridge, this is sailing vessel *Tall Mast*, over."

"*Tall Mast*, Alligator River Bridge. Go ahead."

"Alligator River Bridge, *Tall Mast*. We're the southbound sailboat one mile north of you and request an opening."

"Roger, Captain. Bring her up close and I'll open for you."

"Roger, thank you. This is *Tall Mast* standing by on channel 9."

After you go through the bridge, it's always nice to call the operator back like this: "Alligator River Bridge, *Tall Mast*. Thanks for the opening. This is *Tall Mast* switching back to 16, out."

• Contacting Unknown Vessels to Arrange Safe Passage. As mentioned in the chapter on the Rules of the Road, it's often a good idea to discuss your intentions with another vessel if meeting or overtaking her in constricted waters. Recreational boat operators rarely use sound signals, but call each other on the radio, instead. Traveling the Intracoastal Waterway, which can be quite narrow in places, channel 16 is alive with passing boats hailing each other.

If you can keep your conversation to one or two sentences, you can stay on 16. For example: "*Sweetcakes, Sweetcakes*, this is *Jasmine* directly astern of you. I'd like to pass you on your port side." *Sweetcakes* should come back and say, "Roger, I'll slow." If you need to say more than that, suggest a working channel immediately.

It's easy to hail a vessel when you're directly astern of her and can see the boat's name on the transom. But what about when there's a big ship or a tug a few miles away from you and you want to make sure she sees you? Look on your chart or at your GPS and determine your exact position. Using that information, determine the other vessel's approximate position. Hail her by describing the type of vessel she is, along with her location, then tell her captain where you are. Here are some examples:

o "Calling the outbound Maersk Container Ship that just passed under the Cooper River Bridge, this is motor vessel *Freedom*, two miles off your starboard bow, over."

o "Calling the westbound tug and tow off Sandy Point, this is sailing vessel *Challenger*, one mile off your port bow, over."

o "Calling the northbound oil tanker in approximate position forty degrees twenty-two minutes north, seventy-three degrees forty-five minutes west, this is sailing vessel *Charity* four miles off your starboard beam, over."

Many times the larger ships won't answer you. They often have only one watch stander on the bridge. He may be off grabbing a cup of coffee, or maybe he doesn't speak English well. Whatever the reason, give it another attempt or two. Try on both channel 16 and 13. If there is no answer, take appropriate action to stay out of the vessel's way.

- Calling Towboats. Let's hope you never have to call these guys, but towing companies such as Tow BoatUS or Sea-Tow monitor channel 16. Hail them as you would any other vessel. They'll tell you their working channel so you can discuss your problem there.
- Contacting the Coast Guard. The U.S. Coast Guard monitors channel 16 twenty-four/seven. You would call them in an emergency, certainly (discussed in detail below), but you may also call them with any concerns. Notify them if you see something that may be a hazard to other vessels, such as a buoy that's not where it's supposed to be or a tree floating in the middle of a busy channel.

I'm not sure the following conversation we overheard on channel 16 was a valid reason for calling the Coast Guard, but it certainly provided some entertainment for those of us listening:

Voice: "Coast Guard, Coast Guard, this is *Softie*."

USCG: "*Softie*, this is Coast Guard Station Annapolis."

Voice: "Umm, Coast Guard, I just hit a piling. I didn't see it behind my sail."

USCG: "Sailing Vessel *Softie*, Station Annapolis. Sir, are you in any distress?"

Voice: "No, but there was a bird's nest on top of the piling and I knocked one of the birds onto my deck."

(Pause)

USCG: "*Softie*, this is Coast Guard Station Annapolis. Sir, please shift to our working channel, 22A."

Softie: "Oh. Roger. Shifting to channel 22A."

USCG: "Sailing Vessel *Softie*, this is Coast Guard Station Annapolis on channel 22A."

Softie: "Coast Guard, this is *Softie*. Like I said, there's this baby bird on my deck now, and I don't know what to do with it."

The Coast Guardsman hesitated just long enough for a deep, gravelly voice to cut in and say brusquely, "Eat it."

As I said, people are always listening. The Coast Guard very kindly provided the boater with the phone number of a local wildlife rescue center. *Softie* asked the Coast Guard if they could meet him at the pier and take possession of the bird, but that, obviously, was beyond the scope of their mission.

The Coast Guard is there to help vessels in real distress. Hopefully you will never need to call them for this reason, but like all prudent mariners, it pays to be prepared. Often while taking my turn at the helm, I'll run through in my mind exactly how I would word a distress call if I had to make one at that moment. How would I depict my vessel? How would I describe my location? If you're unsure how to do so, the following section will clear things up.

Distress, Urgency, and Safety Calls

There are three special types of calls with which you should be familiar:

• Mayday: This is used when there is a problem on board the vessel that involves imminent risk of death, serious bodily injury, or loss of the vessel. To make a Mayday call, ensure that your VHF is tuned to channel 16, have your GPS turned to the page with your current position shown, then clearly state the following into the microphone:

o "Mayday, Mayday, Mayday."
o The vessel's name.
o The vessel's description and number of persons aboard.
o The vessel's current location.
o The emergency.

You want to give as much information up-front as possible. You might not be able to hear a reply, but someone on the other end may hear you. So tell them who you are, what you look like, where you are, and what the problem is in one big burst.

After transmitting, await a reply and retransmit as necessary if nothing is heard. Here's how a Mayday call might sound:

"Mayday, Mayday, Mayday. This is motor vessel *Sunshine*. I am a 33-foot, white-hulled cabin cruiser with three people on board, in position thirty-two degrees, forty-six minutes north, seventy-nine degrees, fifty-four minutes west, approximately one mile east of the Battery in Charleston harbor. I am taking on water and request immediate assistance. Over."

When someone replies to your call, simply answer their questions in plain English, ending each transmission with "over."

Do not transmit a Mayday call for non-emergencies. We once overheard a vessel send a call very similar to the example on page 116. The Coast Guard replied immediately and asked if everyone aboard was wearing a life jacket. The vessel in distress responded in the affirmative. The Coast Guard confirmed the boat's position, then asked what the depth of the water was in which the boat was sinking. The reply?

"Two feet."

Hellooooo. Get out of the boat and walk ashore! The Coast Guard was very professional and informed the vessel that they would send someone to assist. They didn't remind them that Mayday calls are reserved for life-threatening situations. In this case, the best type of transmission would have been a Pan-Pan call . . . .

- Pan-Pan (pronounced "pahn-pahn") is an urgency message used to communicate situations that jeopardize the safety of the crew or the vessel, but are not life-threatening. It is a request for assistance and can be worded just like a Mayday call, only you substitute "Pan-Pan" for "Mayday." In general practice, boats requesting Coast Guard assistance when it's not an emergency tend to just call, "U.S. Coast Guard, U.S. Coast Guard, this is So-and-So" on channel 16. The Coast Guard, however, issues Pan-Pan calls quite frequently on behalf of vessels that have requested non-emergency assistance. A typical example is a request to tow a disabled vessel.

- Securité (pronounced "say-cure-eeh-TAY"): When you hear a vessel precede a broadcast with, "Securité, Securité" they are announcing that their intended actions may be of interest to those within listening range of the transmission. A standard call goes like this:

"Securité, Securité. This is tug *Mary Lou*, now departing Sandy Point towing a 200-foot barge astern. (For) all concerned traffic, tug *Mary Lou* standing by on channels 13 and 16. Tug *Mary Lou*, out."

As you can see, a Securité call does not require a response, but it gives listeners an opportunity to contact the caller if there is any concern.

While crossing the mouth of Penobscot Bay, Maine in thick fog, we overheard a tour boat make a Securité call announcing that they were departing a port that was just to the west of us. The vessel was on a course of 110 degrees. I looked at our chart and saw that we would be directly in its path. The captain had ended his call with the standard, "All concerned traffic, standing by on channel 16 and 13."

Well, with visibility at less than 50 feet, I was certainly concerned. I hailed the tour boat on channel 16 and requested that we switch to a working channel. The captain suggested we go to channel 11. Once there, I told him I'd heard his call and I gave him our location. He responded that he could see us on his radar and would remain well clear.

What a great system.

Securité calls aren't just for commercial vessels. If you find yourself in a situation that you want to bring to the attention of those around you, by all means issue a call. For example, at the entrance to Princess Louisa Inlet in British Columbia, there's a cut that's so narrow only one boat can go through at a time. The problem is, the channel curves in such a way that you can't see if anyone's coming from the other direction. The cruising guides advise boaters to issue a Securité call prior to proceeding through the cut, and wisely, they do just that.

HF Radio

Most recreational boats are equipped with VHF radios. Only a small percentage of them—mostly those who plan to go out on the open ocean—carry a high-frequency radio, also known as a single-sideband radio, or SSB. HF radios transmit on a lower frequency than VHF radios (high frequency vs. very high frequency). The lower the frequency, the longer the range. For a blue-water cruiser who needs to communicate economically with stations beyond the range of their VHF radio, a single-sideband radio is the answer. (I say "economically" because today there are satellite phones that will work anywhere in the world, but their per-minute cost is quite high.)

SSBs are not nearly as user-friendly as VHF radios. If you own one, sit down with the manual in front of your set. Learn how all the buttons and dials work and how to use the emergency channels. If you ever need to send a distress signal on 2182 kHz, you'll be glad you took the time to figure out how to do it in advance.

At first the big black radio that came with our boat was a mystery to me. I tried it a few times, but got frustrated when I couldn't do something as simple as dialing in a channel. Then I found a plain-English users' manual on the Internet that took away all the aggravation. Now I use the radio daily to send and receive e-mail.[8] It's a great morale-booster to communicate with family and friends no matter how far we are from land. SSBs are also useful for downloading graphic weather faxes as good as those on your TV's weather channel.

Ham radio operators use HF radio. This requires passing a test to get a license, but it allows boaters to use more frequencies and communicate at any distance around the world.

The Phonetic Alphabet

No radio can compete with Sprint for having a signal so clear you can hear a pin drop. HF reception is usually scratchy no matter where you are. VHF reception worsens the farther you are from the transmitter. The Coast Guard has the tallest antennas and strongest transceivers around, thank goodness, but for those using a standard VHF radio and antenna, the limit is about twenty miles.

---

[8] We have a special modem called a PACTOR III. It links our HF radio with our laptop computer. We use a service called sailmail (www.sailmail.com). Our e-mail goes out over the air through our SSB to one of many sailmail shore stations. They, in turn, forward the messages to the Internet. Isn't modern technology wonderful?

There may come a time when you call someone on your radio and they can't hear you well. They may ask you to spell the name of your vessel or your last name. The best way to ensure they understand your response without their having to ask, "Was that 'f' or 's'?" or "Did you say 'm' or 'n'?" is to use the phonetic alphabet. You'll take all the guesswork out of spelling when you use the following words:

A: Alpha
B: Bravo
C: Charlie
D: Delta
E: Echo
F: Foxtrot
G: Golf
H: Hotel
I: India
J: Juliett
K: Kilo
L: Lima
M: Mike
N: November
O: Oscar
P: Papa (pah-PAH)
Q: Quebec (keh-BECK)
R: Romeo
S: Sierra
T: Tango
U: Uniform
V: Victor
W: Whiskey
X: Xray
Y: Yankee
Z: Zulu

It's not necessary to say "N as in November" or "R as in Romeo." You need only say the respective word for each letter. For example: "Coast Guard Group Hampton, my boat's name is *Liberty*: Lima India Bravo Echo Romeo Tango Yankee. How copy? Over."

Just like other things nautical, you can tell when a person has done their homework. Those who haven't will make up substitutions for the proper names like "N as in Nancy" or "R as in Ricky." You want to sound squared away when you use your radio, so please take five minutes and learn your ABCs all over again.

Oscar Kilo?

Now that you've learned the importance of clear communications and know how to use your marine radio correctly and confidently, this concludes the lesson on communications. If there is no further traffic, this is Suzanne Giesemann switching to the next lesson . . . out.

12

Weather

When you're a landlubber, you turn on the weather channel in the morning to find out what you should wear that day and if you should carry an umbrella. You watch to see if conditions will affect your commute. In most cases, no matter what the weather, you still go about your business.

Maybe you'll check the weather again before going to bed. Other than that, we don't give the weather much thought.

You can avoid bad weather pretty easily when you're on land simply by ducking indoors. It's different on the water. When you're out in a boat, the weather is in your face, sometimes literally. The water can go from flat to lumpy in the snap of your fingers; the wind can change from a gentle whisper to a terrifying roar. It can catch you unawares and leave you scrambling to batten down the hatches and ports.

I'd only been married one week when I learned how quickly weather can change for the worse. I was assigned to supervise a crew of midshipmen on one of the U.S. Naval Academy's 44-foot sloops. We were sailing from Annapolis, Maryland to Portsmouth, New Hampshire and back. We'd gone less than twenty miles on the 2,000-mile voyage when a sudden squall snuck up behind us, grabbed our boom, and slammed it from one side of the boat to the other with frightening force. It was a classic unintentional jibe.

The preventer, a block and tackle device designed to keep the boom from doing exactly what it had just done, blew apart in the strong wind, sending bits of hardware flying in all directions. The force of the boom's slamming across the boat was so strong that the ropes from the preventer fused together around the lifelines and bent one of the boat's stanchions over 45 degrees.

I instructed the midshipman at the helm to steer the boat into the wind, thus relieving the pressure on the mainsail and boom. We straightened out the mess and jury-rigged a new preventer. Not twenty minutes after the potentially life-threatening incident, we were back on track under the same blue skies as we'd started out in. The squall had passed, and everything was back to normal.

Everything, that is, except me. All I wanted to do was go home and curl up next to my new husband. Instead, I had to press on, shaking and shaken, having learned just how powerful Mother Nature can be.

That squall scared the devil out of me, but it taught me a very important lesson that boaters can either learn the hard way, as I did, or read about in a book. I'm going to save you the trauma and let you learn the lesson here. It's quite simple: always keep a weather eye.

That squall didn't just sneak up on us. It blew in on the same winds that had been giving us a great sail until that moment. If we'd turned around and kept watch on the sky, we would have seen the telltale wall of black clouds in time to shorten our sails or take them down altogether.

Forecasts are important, but they can be wrong. The sky, however, doesn't lie. "Keeping a weather eye" means that you constantly have your body's internal radar on, scanning the horizon to watch for anything that foretells a change in the conditions. You pay particular attention to the area upwind. In other words, if the wind is out of the north, watch the sky to the north of you. If the wind is from the east, watch the eastern sky, and so forth. Like a cowboy in a black hat, bad weather rides in on the wind; it doesn't usually go against it.

Knowing what I do now, it's hard to believe that none of us on that 44-footer saw the squall coming. In their defense, the midshipmen were there to learn, and I obviously hadn't learned the lesson yet. None of us noticed the black clouds, or the ripples on the water that foretell approaching wind. Learn from my lesson: watch the sky and the wave tops for changes. No matter what kind of weather is forecast, what you see is what you're going to get. Don't rely on someone else aboard your boat to watch the weather. It's your boat too.

Now that you're going to expand your role aboard your boat, before you get under way you need to make knowledgeable decisions about where and when you should go. Once you're out there, you need to monitor conditions continuously.

In this chapter I'm not going to go into what causes weather and give you a long discussion of the sun, the atmosphere, and global circulation. That's all valuable information and it's readily available. I simply want to make you more aware of how important it is to focus on the weather, and I want to familiarize you with the weather phenomena that you'll see and hear about most often.

You know that there are specific weather channels on your VHF radio. Just as on TV, different stations transmit on different channels, so each of the WX channels on your set covers a different area. Some of the coverage may overlap, though, so dial through them all until you find the best forecast for the area in which you're boating.

Once you start regularly listening to VHF weather forecasts, you'll pick up the pattern of the reports pretty quickly. Most of them give the actual conditions at different locations throughout the listening area, then move on to forecasts for a few days out. The reports include a lot of information. The voice, often electronic, spits out numbers and letters like a machine gun, so have a pen and paper available to make notes. While it's nice to know the temperature, you'll want to pay specific attention to the wind strength, wind direction, and wave height, as well as the possibility of any squalls or thunderstorms.

Wind strength and direction are important to all boaters, not just sailors, because the wind will affect the height and direction of the waves. By listening to the forecast before you go out, you'll know what to expect and can alter your plans accordingly. You may find that the wind and waves will be "on the nose," or coming right from the direction you want to go. It can be pretty miserable to pound into the seas all day long, so you might want to choose a different destination or not go out at all that day.

There are three factors that affect the height of the waves you'll encounter on any given day: how strong the wind is blowing, how long it's been blowing that hard, and how big an area of water the wind has been blowing across. This is known as fetch.

Say the wind is howling through an anchorage you've chosen. Luckily, you're in a tight little cove, so there's not enough fetch to allow any waves to form. Around the point on the open bay, however, the wind has been blowing twenty knots for several days. The waves out there have built up mighty high, and the forecast on your VHF says it's not going to die down for 24 hours. Sounds like a perfect day to stay right where you are and read a good book.

For the most part, the National Weather Service does an excellent job. Be aware, however, that winds are difficult to predict and can exceed those given in the forecast. Conditions can also change rapidly. Listen to the weather on your VHF each time before you get under way, then listen again every hour or two while out on the water.

After digesting the professionals' forecast, add your own observations by watching the clouds and their pattern of formation. You should be able to recognize the different types of clouds and know what they indicate in terms of weather. Find a book with photos of clouds so you can identify them more easily. We have one aboard *Liberty*, and it actually helped settle a squabble between my husband and me . . . .

Most people look at clouds and see shapes. You know: bunny rabbits, horses, that sort of thing. Not my Ty. On the day in question, he pointed at the sky and said, "Hey, look at those clouds. They look just like a bunch of breasts." I couldn't help but roll my eyes and make a comment about men and their one-track minds. He looked suitably insulted and went below. A moment later he emerged with our cloud book in hand and a triumphant smile on his face.

"Look," he said, pointing to a photo of a sky that looked exactly like the one above us. "I'm not the only one who thinks this way."

Sure enough, the heading on the page was, "Mamma Clouds," and the description read, "The pouches appear on the cloud after or towards the end of the storm and are called mamma from their obvious resemblance to breasts."[9]

Son of a gun.

While mamma clouds are of particular interest to my husband, the following are important to you as a boater:

Cirrus are the thin ones that are very high in the sky. They're the first sign that a warm front may be approaching, bringing rain or a storm with it. The good news is, when you see those wispy clouds, you usually have 24 to 48 hours to take shelter. If the sky is full of cirrus clouds and they start to form ripples, known as a mackerel sky, a storm may be much closer than a day away.

As a warm front approaches, the different types of clouds keep getting lower and lower in the sky. Nimbostratus are the thick, heavy,

[9] Lawrence, Eleanor and Van Loon, Borin. *An Instant Guide to Weather*, Gramercy Books, New York, 1999, p. 55.

gray clouds that often have a jagged lower edge. Nimbostratus have their base at about 3,000 feet and build up higher from there. They're your basic rain cloud.

Cumulus are the fluffy white clouds that look like cotton balls. They're always a welcome sight, because they float around up there on bright, sunny days. It's when those little puffy clouds start clumping together and getting bigger and bigger that you need to take notice.

Cumulonimbus form from big cumulus clouds. They pile up and up, growing very high, and their top edge can become flat like an anvil. Watch out for those anvils. Even though most of the cloud is white, the base is often gray. These clouds can bring nasty thunderstorms with heavy rain and sometimes hail. Steer clear of them.

The lowest type of cloud is fog. Yes, fog is nothing more than clouds at ground level. Unless you have radar on board and are skilled at using it, you may want to stay in port if fog is in the forecast.

I got a real kick out of sailing in Nova Scotia, where fog is a regular occurrence. Just as we had done back in the States, we listened to the weather every day. No matter what the forecast, Environment Canada gave the same warning: "Visibility will be fair in rain and poor in fog."

What an amazing grasp of the obvious.

Your VHF isn't the only place to get reliable forecasts. The Internet abounds with weather sites for the mariner. The National Weather Service has one of the best, included as part of the National Oceanographic and Atmospheric Agency's (NOAA) site. Check out www.nws.noaa.gov for both graphic and text versions of the latest forecasts.

Many marinas will post weather maps near the office, where you can see what's in store for you graphically. The problem with the Internet and maps posted on bulletin boards is that they can seem like a bunch of hieroglyphics if you don't know what you're looking at.

Any basic weather book will include a chart to explain the symbols used on weather maps. With a little study and practice, you'll be able to read the maps and predict the weather just like a meteorologist. Several things will jump out at you when you look at a weather map. These include: big Ls and Hs inside concentric circles, curving lines with circles or triangles on them, big numbers, and little arrows, like this:

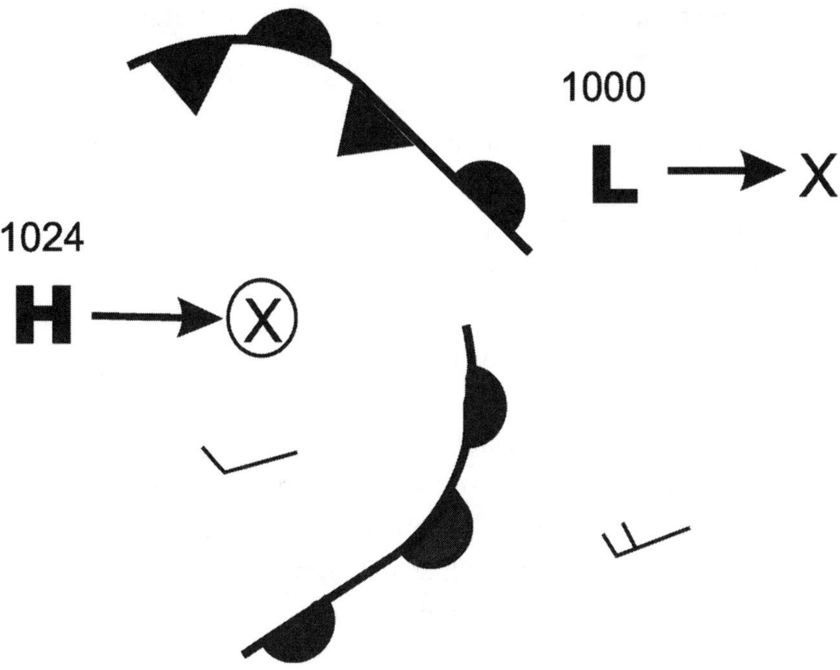

You'll hear forecasters talk about lows and highs moving into your area. These low and high pressure systems are large areas of similar barometric pressure that bring changes in the weather as you transition from one system to another.

A big L on a weather map indicates a low-pressure system, while an H represents a high. The average barometric pressure is 1013 millibars, the unit of measure for atmospheric pressure. So when you're in the middle of a low-pressure system, your barometer will show readings of around 1000 or below. Highs in North America usually show barometric readings around 1020 and above.

In general, low is bad and high is good. See how simple this is? Lows are associated with rain, low clouds, and possibly fog—your typical gray, dreary day. Highs bring blue, sunny skies and generally settled weather with clear visibility. If you look at a weather map and there's a great big H right over your position, you know you're in for a nice day.

The concentric circles or rings around the Ls and Hs are lines of equal barometric pressure. Anywhere on a given ring, the barometric pressure is the same. The National Weather Service builds its weather charts by compiling data from thousands of stations across the area covered. When all these stations report the barometric pressure at their location, those concentric circles simply "connect the dots" where the pressures are the same.

Those open-ended curving lines on weather maps indicate fronts. A front is an area where large air masses of different temperature and/or moisture conditions meet. The term was first used in a meteorological sense during World War I by likening a front to a battlefront. Why? Because most unsettled weather and some of the most violent conditions occur at fronts.

The little half-circles along a frontal line indicate a warm front. Pointed triangles are used for cold fronts. This is easy to remember if you think that certain body parts get pointy when it's cold. (Ok, ok, I know... now who's thinking about breasts?) A line with alternating triangles and half-circles on different sides of the line is a stationary front—one that's just lingering and not going anywhere. When you see this symbology, think of Dr. Doolittle's "Push-Me-Pull-You." An occluded front occurs when a cold front rides up over a warm front, so the symbology will show half-circles and triangles on the same side of the line. You'll generally find rain both in front of and behind these nasty fronts.

Now you understand the symbols, but what do they mean to you as a boater?

Most weather systems in the northern hemisphere move from west to east. If the frontal line on the weather map you're looking at is to the west of your current position, the front may be headed your way. Look closely at the map. NOAA charts include an arrow coming off the Low or High indicating what direction the system is expected to move. The arrow usually ends with an X to show where they expect the Low or High to be 24 hours from the time shown on the map you're looking at.

If you see a front headed your way, here's what you can expect before, during, and after its passage:

• Warm fronts. As a warm front approaches, the wind will start to increase. It will probably be raining continuously, and as the Canadians will tell you, "visibility will be fair." As the front passes over you, the wind will shift in a clockwise direction and possibly decrease in strength. Precipitation may stop, but visibility may still be limited by mist or fog. After the warm front passes, the winds will steady out in both strength and direction. Light drizzle may remain for a while, and visibility will be fair to poor, especially if fog persists.

• Cold fronts. Before a cold front reaches you, the winds will increase and the weather may be squally. You may have a little rain and thunder with associated poor visibility. Cold fronts move about twice as fast as warm fronts, so things happen faster and more violently. As the front passes over, you'll experience a sudden clockwise shift in the wind, with more squalls likely. Expect heavy rain accompanied by thunder. You may even get some hail. After the front passes, the wind will still be gusty for a little while. You may have heavy rain for a short time, then see fair skies with scattered showers possible. Obviously, visibility will then be very good, except in the showers.

Keeping in mind that these are generalizations, warm fronts usually occur on the east side of low-pressure systems. They travel at about 12-15 knots. Cold fronts follow warm fronts within the same low, but at a much faster speed, anywhere between 10 and 50 knots. This difference in speed between warm and cold fronts is why you can get those occluded fronts where the cold air catches up and rides over the warm.

Because of their higher speeds, cold fronts tend to bring violent weather, but for a short time. After a cold front passes, you'll often feel a noticeable drop in the temperature.

Now you know what those front lines on weather maps mean to you as a boater. That rapid-fire voice on your VHF will take on more meaning, as well. If the report says, "A strong cold front will move through the area late this afternoon," beware. If it tells you that "a warm front will linger over the area for several days," you might want to have your foul-weather gear ready.

You should also know about the arrows scattered over weather maps. Like the kind of arrow you shoot, they have little fleches at the back end, but they don't have points at the front; nevertheless, the straight (though unpointed) end indicates the direction the wind is blowing. The fleches tell you the wind strength. Short fleches indicate winds of 5 knots, long fleches equal ten knots. So an arrow with two long fleches and one short means that in that area the winds are blowing 25 knots in the direction the tip-less arrow is pointing. Once the winds reach 50 knots, the fleches are replaced with a triangle.

You don't want to see triangles.

Take a close look at a weather map and you'll see that there's a predictable pattern to the arrows. In the northern hemisphere, winds associated with low-pressure systems flow counterclockwise. High-pressure systems are just the opposite, with winds flowing clockwise around the center. By looking at the arrows for the area in which you want to take your boat, you'll know how strong you can expect the winds to be and from what direction they'll be blowing.

Once you break down those confusing maps into their component parts, they're not so mysterious after all. When you see how important it is to know the wind strength and direction, or that a front is coming your way, or whether you're going to be traveling through a high or low pressure system, you pay a little more attention.

And that's the bottom line. As a boater, you need to show far more interest in the weather than a landlubber. It will directly affect not just your comfort and enjoyment, but your safety as well.

Competent mariners don't ignore the weather. They pay attention to forecasts and keep a weather eye. It's the prudent thing to do. After all, as my father taught me when I was growing up, "Whether it's cold or whether it's hot, you're going to have weather, whether or not."

13

Line Handling

If you're like most women afloat, you handle the lines while your partner docks the boat. If so, you may already be familiar with the information in this chapter. But just in case you're new to boating or haven't yet learned all the nifty knots and valuable safety lessons, I encourage you to review this important aspect of boating.

And you bet it's important. Just because men often shunt line-handling duties off on women doesn't mean it's not a critical skill. Think about it—you can't just pull your boat into a slip and set the parking brake. Failure to handle lines and secure your boat properly can easily result in dings and scratches to your boat's nice finish. Or worse.

Did you notice I used the word "skill?" Handling lines is exactly that. A skill is something that must be learned and takes practice. If not used frequently, it gets rusty. Sounds like line handling to me. If you haven't tied a clove hitch or cleated off a line in a while, your fumbling fingers will let you know just how much skill is required. Even though you're going to be doing more of the driving and docking after you finish this book, you'll want to maintain your proficiency with lines.

So with "Safety First" as our motto, we'll begin with line safety.

I clearly remember the day we docked at Norfolk's Waterside Marina. Two employees met us at our slip to catch the lines. They wore shirts to identify themselves as staff members, and when they turned around to leave, I couldn't help but laugh. Across their backs in large letters were the words "Human Fender."

Their boss must have had a great sense of humor. But he was smart, too. Those shirts, while humorous, surely delivered a continuous subliminal message to the staff. It's a message you, too, will be wise to remember: Never put any body parts between your boat and another object. Even if the boat's about to crunch against a piling or a dock, gel coat is far more repairable than an arm or leg.

Dock lines are strong. They're designed to take a lot of strain. Your back isn't. When controlling a boat with lines, let the lines do all the work. Don't stand there and pull directly on a line that's attached to a multi-ton vessel. Always put a line around a cleat, piling, or bollard[10] first, then take a strain on it.

It's the nature of lines to kink and curl. Those little loops that form when a line curls around itself are called bights. Before taking a strain on a line, make sure you're not standing in the bight of the line. Not only could this be painful, but it could also pull you right into the water.

Speaking of strain, some day you may play Good Samaritan and give a tow to another boat. Or perhaps you might find yourself on the unhappy end of a towing line. In either case, stay clear of the towing line. There's a tremendous amount of tension on a line under strain, especially one that's towing several thousand pounds of boat. If a towing line were to part, it would snap back in the direction the line is coming from with potentially harmful consequences. Resist the temp-

---

[10] A bollard is a short, vertical, square or rounded post used for securing lines.

tation to stand up there at the bow and keep an eye on things. You can do just as good a job observing from the protection of your cockpit.

If you're on a sailboat, be mindful when using winches. The wind can unexpectedly fill a sail, pulling the line taut. Heaven forbid your fingers should get caught between the line and the winch. The best way to prevent this from happening is to modify the way you hold a line when wrapping it around the winch.

Pick up the line you're going to wrap around a winch by holding your dominant hand out like a hitchhiker. As you wrap the line around the winch, always wrap in a clockwise direction. Keep the heel of your hand facing the winch. Rotate your wrist as you go so that your thumb is pointing outwards at all times.

Make the hitchhiker sign with your hand now so you see what I mean. If the sail were to pull the line taut, taking your hand with it, the highly padded heel of your hand would thump almost painlessly against the winch. Now hold your hand out like most people hold lines. What's going to jam into the winch if there's a sudden strain in the line? Your highly breakable thumb and forefinger. The hitchhiker way of holding a line is a nifty little trick that will probably feel awkward at first, like when your parents showed you how to hold a fork the right way. After you do it a few times it won't seem so strange, and you'll see the logic in it.

When using a winch, take at least three wraps around it before grinding in the line. This will prevent the line from slipping. When it comes time to ease the line, place the palm of one hand flat against the wraps on the drum as you let the line out with the other hand. This maintains positive control of the line and provides a braking action.

All this talk about stress, strain, and body parts isn't meant to frighten you. Like anything else, when handled correctly and with due respect, lines will do exactly what they're designed to do, and do it safely.

There are two primary types of line: double braid and three-strand. Double braid appears woven, while three-strand is twisted and looks like a candy cane. Double braid doesn't stretch much, so it's perfect for running rigging on sailboats—those sheets and halyards used to adjust sails. You don't want running rigging to stretch, or you'd have to keep adjusting your sails.

You do want dock lines and anchor lines to stretch. In this case, the stretching acts like a shock absorber. That's why three-strand, being stretchier, more resistant to abrasion, and cheaper, is great for dock and anchor lines. Nevertheless, double braid is softer and more flexible than three-strand. It's easier to handle and coil, plus it's 15 percent stronger, so some boaters use double braid for dock lines as well.

You can tell a squared-away boat at first glance by how the owners coil their lines. If the running rigging and dock lines are carelessly lying on the deck, that's a sign that other things on the boat may not be well attended either. Take pride in your boat and your lines. Coil the "leftover" end into a circle or concentric rows on the deck or dock. Coiling a line allows the line to run free when you need it.

You can also wrap excess line into a neat bundle, then wrap the bitter end around the coil and through the resultant loop at the end to secure it. Double braid line should be looped in figure eights to keep it from kinking. No matter what kind of line you use, always start coiling from the standing end—the part that's attached to something—and not the bitter, or loose end. These methods not only look good, but they also eliminate trip hazards.

It's a good idea to have a loose coil of line in hand as your boat approaches a dock. Make sure that it leads outside all lifelines and standing rigging. If you're lucky, someone will be standing on the dock ready to grab your lines for you. In that case, keep the standing end of the line (the part attached to the boat) in your non-dominant hand and toss the coil of line with your dominant hand. This is not the time to be timid, nor is it good to jump the gun. It's always frustrating, not to mention embarrassing and stressful, to watch your line fall into the water. Be patient and wait until you're sure you're closer than the length of your dock line, then give it a nice, confident toss.

Many times you'll have to secure your boat without assistance. Resist the urge to jump onto a dock. Step ashore with line in hand only when it's safe. The most common piece of hardware to which you secure dock lines is a two-horned cleat. You should be able to wrap a line around a cleat and release it equally quickly. When cleating a line, always run it to the far end of the cleat first. Take a wrap under the horn, then over and under both horns. Lock the line by passing it under the last loop you made. It's not necessary to make multiple figure eights. A round turn and two figure eights is sufficient and makes it easier to undo in a hurry.

If you attach a line to a cleat simply by passing a loop over it, make sure the other end is cleated. If both ends of the same line are attached with loops, it will be next to impossible to get the line free when under strain. If one end is cleated, you can ease the line little by little.

There are four types of lines for securing a boat: bow, stern, spring, and breast. If you simply take lines from the bow and stern to the dock, your boat can still move around. That's where spring lines come in. They keep your boat from "springing" forward and aft. A breast line runs straight across from midships on the boat and keeps you from moving laterally away from the pier. In that sense, bow and stern lines that run perpendicular to the boat could also be considered breast lines.

Before you even approach a pier or slip, figure out which way you'll first need to stop your boat from moving. Are the wind and/or current coming from ahead? Get your bow line or aft spring line (the one going from the bow and leading aft) over first. Are they pushing you in from astern? Secure your stern line or forward spring first. If the wind is blowing perpendicular to the pier and away from it, get your midships breast line over first, if you're close enough.

No lesson on line handling would be complete without a section on knots. Once again, entire books are dedicated to this topic, complete with fancy diagrams to show you how to tie all kinds. You can get by quite well with about five basic knots. I advise you to learn them now, before you need them in a pinch.

I was sitting in my cockpit at a marina in Florida when I noticed a large boat heading for the slip next to ours. One of the unwritten rules among boaters is to always assist someone with their dock lines unless it would hazard what you're doing. Reading a book didn't qualify as a hazard, so I jumped up to help.

Theirs was the end slip. The only thing between our two boats was a large piling. The finger pier was this stubby little thing up at the bow that was no help whatsoever. All I could do was stand on my own deck and offer to catch their lines. The wind was blowing about 18 knots, pushing the boat away from the piling closest to me and onto the one on their far side. It was crucial to get a line around the windward piling as quickly as possible.

As usual, the man was at the helm. The woman stood on deck with a nervous frown on her face and tossed me a stern line. It fell far short and splashed into the water. The line just wasn't long enough to get all the way over to me so I could hold them off the leeward piling. She did have enough line to get around the piling, and that was the important thing.

Because the piling was so tall, she needed to put a big loop in it and help it over with a boat hook. Sensing that the woman didn't know what to do, I shouted, "Tie a bowline in it to form a loop."

If she seemed anxious before, now she froze. Her arms hung uselessly at her sides, and she said, "I don't know how to tie a bowline."

By now the boat was pinned against the far pilings. Her husband called her over and told her to push the boat off while he tied a bowline in the dock line. Once he looped it around the piling, they were able to center the boat in the slip.

The tension in the air was rather thick as they secured the rest of their lines. I felt sorry for the woman, but the whole scene could have been avoided if she'd known how to tie one of the most basic knots in boating.

A bowline forms a loop in the end of a line. It's extremely strong, yet no matter how much strain is put on a line, it never jams. You can always break (untie) the knot by bending it.

As you tie a bowline, you choose how large or small to make the loop. If you don't make the loop big enough, you can pass the rest of the line through the initial loop you made to instantly form an even bigger loop. Loops formed by bowlines are useful for placing over pilings, cleats, and bollards or for tying off a dinghy painter to a rail. You can tie two lines together using a bowline in the end of each one. Loop the second line through the first bowline before tying the second bowline.

Here's how a correctly tied bowline should look:

Many people find bowlines tricky. It's easy to forget how to make them unless you practice and use them often. You should be able to tie a bowline quickly and in the dark, so whenever you have a minute and your hands are idle, practice tying a bowline, then do it again with your eyes closed.

The remaining four knots are even easier than a bowline:

• Clove hitch: great for tying fenders to a toe rail or lifeline or for wrapping a dock line around a piling. It's easy to tie, to adjust, and to untie.

• Half hitch: a good knot to tie after you've put a clove hitch in a line to keep it from slipping. You can make just one half hitch, or two in a row for extra security.

• Figure eight, also known as a "stopper knot" for its most common use: to stop lines from getting away from you. After you run a line through a block or eye or through the center of a cleat, it's a good practice to always put a figure eight in the end. I've lost track of the number of times a jib sheet has slipped out of my hands and gone running off down the deck. If it weren't for the stopper knot it would have gone in the water or become a whip. Instead, it stopped when it came to a piece of hardware smaller than the knot. Take a tour around your boat and check all running rigging for stopper knots. If they're not there, put them in.

• Square knot: useful for tying two lines of equal dimension together. Tying a square knot is similar to tying your shoes. You start with a line in each hand. Cross one line over and under the other and pull a bit to tighten. Now, instead of making loops as you would when tying your shoes, cross the lines over and under again. This time, however, cross the opposite line from the one you started with over and under the other and tighten. For example, if you first crossed over and under with the left line, this time go over and under with the right line. If you first went over and under with the right line, the second time go over and under with the left line. The result should look like the knot above. If you don't reverse the direction in which you cross the lines, you'll end up with a granny knot. Granny knots are no good because they always slip. Try it and see. If you make what you think is a square knot, but it comes apart when you pull on both ends, you crossed both lines in the same direction, Granny.

Knowing how to tie these five knots correctly will save you time and effort. We had a guest join us while cruising the Bahamas. Tom was a fellow sailor and was eager to pitch in. When we got under way from the pier in Marsh Harbor, he asked what he could do to help. I was at the helm, so I asked him to take in the fenders and hang them horizontally along the stern rail. (Note that the sooner you take in your fenders, the sooner you'll look shipshape and all lines will be out of the water).

Tom asked how we normally hang our fenders, and I said, "Just tie a simple clove hitch and let the rest of the line hang down."

I heard him utter "...a simple clove hitch" as he turned away. The funny look on his face told me that maybe it wasn't simple to everyone.

Until that point, Tom hadn't needed to use a clove hitch because the fenders on his boat had plastic hangers that allowed him to simply slip them over the lifelines. This is a prime example of how time-saving gadgets can keep you from learning necessary skills.

We sailed around all day, then went to a marina at Great Guana Cay. By this time Tom was at the helm, so I went aft to ready the fenders. I reached for the first line and stopped in my tracks. Staring back at me was a series of hitches, bends, and unidentifiable knots. It took me a good minute and a half to untie just the first line.

With seven lines to go—two each on four fenders—I decided it was best if I let the man who tied the knots untie them as well. I asked Tom if he'd mind rigging fenders while I took the helm. He eagerly agreed, and I smiled to myself as he pulled apart knot after knot after knot.

When we got under way the next day, I made a point of taking in the fenders and attaching them in our normal way. Tom watched attentively. After another glorious afternoon of sailing, Tom jumped to ready the fenders; I watched him out of the corner of my eye. With only a simple clove hitch in the lines, he was able to release them in seconds. I could almost see the light bulb go on over his head. He was a quick study, and as you can guess, the next time he hung the fenders, his clove hitches were perfect.

Working with lines is both a science and an art that dates back through the centuries. When you can tie a bowline as easily as you lace your shoes and cleat a line as effortlessly as a cowboy ropes a calf, you'll know you've joined the ranks of thousands who've gone to sea before you. Hone your skills, sailor, and take pride in them.

14

Boat Handling and Docking

Have you ever single-handed your boat? You know, taken it out with no one else aboard? If your reaction is something along the lines of, "Who me? Are you kidding?" you might want to reconsider. It's not a bad idea to be prepared to handle your boat all by yourself, just in case you someday find yourself alone at the helm.

If it sounds as if I'm speaking from experience, I am.

It had been a long winter. We hadn't been under way in four months. We'd stayed aboard a few times, though, and now that spring had arrived, our first order of business was a trip to the pump-out pier.

Since Ty and I share the docking fifty-fifty, we had to decide who would drive. Neither of us could remember who docked the boat at the end of the last season, so Ty offered to let me take her out.

I was up for the challenge and stepped to the helm. We hadn't owned our 46-footer long, but it was long enough to learn that she backed like a bicycle, rarely going where I wanted her to.

This day, however, she surprised me by backing beautifully to starboard, allowing me to pull ahead and drive straight down the narrow fairway between piers. Once in the main marina channel, I tested the wheel. It felt strange in my hands, slow to respond. I looked behind me at the aft deck. The transom seemed especially far away. This boat was ten feet longer than our previous one, and I still wasn't used to her.

I turned toward the pump-out pier and planned my approach. There wasn't much current, but the wind would be blowing me off the dock. I'd have to come in flat, instead of at an angle. Ty had lines and fenders rigged to port. He stood by the gate in the lifelines, ready to cleat us off.

What is it they say about the "best laid plans?"

As I pulled up to the pier, Ty stepped onto the dock and cleated off the stern line. Before he could run forward and grab the bow line, however, the wind took control and pushed the bow out. The boat was now lying completely perpendicular to the pier.

I ran forward to try to toss Ty the bow line, but it was too short to reach the pier from that angle. Ty reacted by uncleating the stern line and tossing it back onto the boat. There I stood on the deck with my husband on the pier shouting, "Take her around again!"

Easy for him to say.

Suddenly I was a single-hander, with no choice but to do exactly what he said and take her around again. The approach to the pier looked wide and roomy, but I knew the channel had shoals on both sides. I motored away a safe distance, then backed and filled—going forward and in reverse like turning a car in a three-point turn—until I was once again facing the pier.

Turning my eyes skyward, I said a quick prayer, then headed in. Now I knew exactly how the wind would affect the landing, so I went just a bit faster than before. I came in flat like the first time, but closer now, and backed her down to stop. After putting the engine in neutral, I ran forward and tossed Ty the bow line, then scurried aft and did the same with the stern line. We were secured.

The tension I'd felt minutes earlier was replaced with tremendous pride. I'd done it.

Docking is rarely stress free. There's always that element of "what could go wrong?" because a boat doesn't handle like a car. You can't step on a brake and stop in an instant. A boat doesn't only move forward and backward, it moves sideways, too—sometimes when you wish it wouldn't. Boats also turn differently than cars and take longer to do so.

What happened to me at the pump-out pier could just as easily have happened to Ty. He would have had to take her around again, too. I only did what any boat owner would do and should be able to do, if for no other reason than for safety.

We women need to get over the fear of handling a boat, and assume the same responsibility for driving and docking as a man. If we're going to be boat owners, we should be boat operators, as well.

This includes driving a dinghy, if you own one. Starting an outboard engine is no more difficult than starting a lawn mower. After just a few minutes of instruction, you can zip around the harbor with the same independence you enjoy on land. Don't wait for your partner to take you when you want to go ashore. Drive yourself. But one word of advice: If your outboard engine comes with a little cord attached to a "kill switch," never get under way, even if it's to visit the boat next to yours, without wrapping that cord around your wrist. Should you ever get dumped out of the dinghy, the cord will pull out, and the engine will instantly stop. I've heard tragic stories of people being sliced by their own propellers because they didn't use this critical piece of safety gear.

As for docking, every time Ty and I see a boat entering or departing a marina with a woman at the helm, we point it out to each other. We comment about it because it's such a rare sight. I'll bet you do the same. At the very least, you take notice.

What a shame that a woman docking a boat is an oddity. I used to think the percentages would at least be higher among cruising women who spend more time on their boats. This belief was disavowed one day when I brought our boat alongside the fuel pier at Green Turtle Cay in the Abacos.

As Ty tossed our bow lines to the dock hand, the young man asked, "Who's driving the boat?"

Ty answered, "My wife."

The man's eyes widened and he said, "A woman?"

Well, I hope so.

He told us he'd never seen a woman dock a boat. Think about that. This was someone who worked at a busy fuel pier at a major cruising destination. It was a telling moment.

I think I can safely assume that you drive a car. It's rare to find a woman who relies on her partner to drive her everywhere, unless there's a medical reason. Yes, by culture and tradition, if a man and woman go for a short ride together, more often than not the man will take the wheel. But the woman could just as easily drive, and very often does so.

Why is it so drastically different with boats? I'm specifically talking about docking, because that's when most women turn over the wheel to their partner. They may take the helm all day out in open water, but when it comes time to return to the pier, suddenly it's hands-off.

If you recognize yourself here, at least you're not alone. But that's no excuse for depriving yourself of a skill that's as much a part of boating as making sure the galley is well stocked—and it's a heck of a lot more fun.

The most common excuses I hear from women as to why they don't dock their boats include:

- "My husband always does it." (This is an excuse?)
- "My husband won't let me." (Won't let you? Please review the chapter on your role aboard your boat.)
- "It makes me nervous." (Guess what? It probably makes your partner nervous when he does it, too.)
- "I've never done it before" or "I don't know how." (You had to learn how to drive a car, right? Parallel parking and three-point turns didn't just come naturally. Maneuvering a boat may be a bit more complicated, but like driving, it's a learned skill.)

What say you learn?

For the sake of this discussion, I'm going to talk about "taking the wheel" or "turning the wheel." If you use a tiller, don't worry. I'm mostly concerned here with maneuvering, and that will be the same for boats with wheels or tillers.

How many propellers does your boat have? Most larger powerboats have two, while trawlers and sailboats only have one. Lucky you if you have two, as "twin screws" make maneuvering in tight spaces far easier. By putting one engine in forward and the other in reverse, you can turn, or twist, the boat in place.[11] Those with a single engine

[11] A great way to understand turning with two engines is to stand with your hands on your hips, elbows out to the side. If you turn left, which elbow goes forward and which goes back? And if you turn right? That's exactly how you work the engines on a twin-screw boat: one goes forward and one goes back,

have to do a lot of backing and filling to turn their boats around. Getting into tight places is far more of a challenge with one prop than with two.

Before you even attempt to dock your boat, you first want to learn how your boat reacts when you put it in forward and reverse. Well, duh—it goes forward or backward, right? Thank you. I'm talking about maneuvering with finesse here, ladies.

Choose a day with little wind. Find someone whose boat handling skills you trust and with whom you're comfortable to go along. Maybe that's your partner, and maybe it isn't. In any case, take your boat out to a wide, open area with plenty of deep water in all directions and an object of reference nearby, such as a boat at anchor or a float.

Practice pulling alongside the object, staying about three boat lengths away, then bring your boat to a stop. Put the engine in forward and slowly pull ahead. This slow motion is called idle. Many throttles click into place in idle position. Observe how fast your boat moves when it's in idle.

Now stop the boat. Remember, this is not like a car. You do not have brakes. To stop a boat that's moving forward, put it in reverse until you take the way off. To stop a boat that's backing, do the opposite and put the boat in forward gear. The more juice you give it, the faster it will stop. Listen to your engine. Watch the response in relation to your nearby object. How much throttle do you need for these small maneuvers? How does your engine sound when you're in neutral? In idle? Sound plays an important role in driving a boat.

Now that you've pulled ahead of your reference object, put the engine in reverse and back slowly until you're lined up again. Stop there and hold it. Make minor adjustments to keep her in place. If you start to skew a little, straighten the boat by "goosing" the engine. To do this, put the engine in neutral, turn the wheel in the direction you want the bow to move, then put the engine in gear and give the throttle a quick rev. You know: "Vroom." After that one quick burst, immediately go back into neutral. The bow will move where you want it to with next to no forward motion.

How cool is that?

When you've straightened out again, bring the wheel back amidships (center your rudder).

I really want you to do these things. Don't just read about them. Every boat handles differently. The only way you'll learn how your boat handles is by actually handling it. The time you invest in familiarizing yourself with your boat will pay off like three-of-a-kind on a slot machine when it comes time to maneuver in tight spaces.

Whether driving the boat in close quarters or on open water, avoid giving your boat more helm than it needs. Most boats don't react as instantaneously as cars when you turn the wheel. That water they're floating in adds a certain amount of resistance. Figure in that slow reaction time and have patience. She'll come around.

If you use too much helm, you'll find yourself overcorrecting—turning the wheel one way then the other until the boat starts skewing back and forth. If this happens, take a deep breath and stop steering for a moment. Wait and see which way the bow turns, then slowly bring her back on course. Continue steering now, but turn the wheel as little as possible.

Now you're getting a good feel for how your boat reacts to engine and rudder changes. You should be having fun. If not, check your attitude. There's no danger of hitting anything. You're in control and you know what you're doing. Time to push that comfort zone just a little bit. Yes, it's time to practice docking.

Oh no. I could feel the tension rising at the mere mention of the D-word. That's a natural reaction, but you're not going to give in to your fears this time. You're going to learn to dock just like you learned to drive a car. Welcome back to Drivers' Ed., my friend.

As with most instruction, the theory comes before the hands-on practice. Understanding the factors that affect how your boat moves will help you to anticipate what's going to happen when you go through the various docking scenarios.

The two things that every boater should consider before leaving or returning to a marina are wind and current.[12] Both have the potential to push your boat around in ways you neither intended nor desire. Your goal is to correctly anticipate and compensate for wind and current in such a manner that the boat goes exactly where you want it to.

With these two factors in mind, there are four questions you should ask yourself every time before you make a move in or out of a slip:

1. How will the wind affect me?
2. How will the current affect me?
3. Which will have the greater effect on my maneuvering?
4. How should I compensate for these effects?

Assessing wind and current is so critical to a successful docking evolution that I want to repeat myself: Commit these questions to memory and ask them every time before docking. Even if you always leave from and return to the same slip, the wind and current are constantly changing. Your boat will react differently each time, so let's look at each one of the four questions in detail.

1. How will the wind affect me?

What is the wind strength? If your boat has a lot of freeboard, wind will be more of a consideration for you than for other boats. For any boat, winds under about 8 knots won't be much of a concern when

---

[12] We'll assume that depth is not an issue, as that's something you check no matter where you're maneuvering.

docking. If the wind is blowing 8-15 knots, you're likely to feel the effects of it. Winds from 15-20 will definitely push you around some, and if it's blowing more than 20, you may want to consider staying put.

What direction is the wind blowing? You can determine wind speed and direction in two ways: with electronic wind speed and direction instruments aboard your boat (more often found on sailboats than power), and by personal observation. Look at the flags on nearby vessels or at your own. Which way are they blowing and how hard are they flapping? If there are trees nearby, observe how their branches and leaves move. That's the direction the wind will push your boat as you leave or enter your dock.

2. How will the current affect me?

Tides cause current. Water flows in from the sea and back out again as it floods and ebbs. Tidal current takes a while to pick up speed, with the fastest flow occurring right in the middle of a low or high tide. This is called maximum flood or maximum ebb. The speed of this current varies from location to location. You should find out how fast the current runs at max flood or ebb where you keep your boat as well as where you are each time you dock in a different place.

The period just before a tide reverses or starts to flow again has the slowest current. For a short period of time—about half an hour right on either side of high tide and low tide—there's no tidal flow at all. This is called slack water and is the best time for docking maneuvers.

How can you tell how strong the current is and which way it's flowing? Two ways. First, consult your tide tables. Where are you in the normal ebb and flow of tide? At max ebb or max flood? At slack water, or somewhere in between? Know which direction the current flows where you are when it's flooding and ebbing. Some books like *Reed's Nautical Almanac* contain tidal current tables that eliminate the guesswork.

Second, look at the water. If your boat is stopped, observe how quickly bubbles or floating objects like leaves or sticks are flowing past. What direction are they moving? Look at the tail in the water left by the current behind objects like pilings or buoys. Sometimes the current is so strong that a buoy will lean way over. That's the direction the current will push your boat as you're maneuvering.

3. Which will have the greater effect on my maneuvering?

First, know your boat. In general, if you have a lot of freeboard and a shallow keel, wind will affect you more than current. If your boat has a deep keel running the length of the boat, but low topsides, current may be more of a factor. All things being equal, whichever is stronger, current or wind, will be your main concern. Keep in mind that four knots of current is not the same as four knots of wind.

Let me use Charleston again as an example. At max flood and ebb, there's about a four-knot current running through the harbor. That's pretty fast. A four-knot current is strong enough to overcome even a moderately strong wind. You can see this effect and immediately tell which way the current is going simply by looking at the boats at anchor by the Ashley River highway bridge. In most places, boats at anchor lie bow-to-the-wind. Not so in Charleston.

When the tide is flooding, or going from low to high (Filling in the river from sea), all the boats at anchor are pointed into the current. Once the tide turns and the river begins to ebb (Empty out to sea), going from high to low tide, all the boats march around in unison and point the other way—into that four-knot current. It takes a really strong wind to counteract a current that strong.

This is an extreme example. Most anchorages don't have such strong currents, so boats at anchor will usually be more affected by the wind than current. When docking, you'll need to compensate for whichever has the stronger effect on your boat, given the conditions.

4. How should I compensate for these effects?

Look at the way your slip is oriented to the wind and current flow. Will one or the other be pushing you off the pier or onto it? If onto it, you can let the external factors do some of your work for you. Come in a bit slower than usual. You can even stop before you get to the dock. Then let the wind or current gently nudge you until your fenders softly cushion your landing.

Ahhhhh.

If you'll be pushed away from the pier by wind or current, have dock lines ready, then use a little more speed than normal. Bring the boat as close to the pier as possible, and get those lines over right away.

There's one more bit of theory I want to discuss before we move on to actual docking practice. If you have a boat with a rudder, instead of a boat that steers strictly by turning an outboard engine, know that a rudder has far more effect when water is being pushed across it. Propellers are always placed forward of the rudder so that as the prop turns, it's also pushing water directly onto the rudder. Because of this, your rudder "bites" into the water much better. You'll have far more steering control when your engine is engaged than when you're simply drifting along in neutral. This is especially important to remember when maneuvering in tight quarters. If you want more control, put your boat in gear instead of just drifting in neutral.

Whether your boat has a rudder or not, you may be affected by a phenomenon known as prop walk. Most boats' propellers turn clockwise when the boat's going forward. When the engine is put in reverse, the propeller turns the other way (unless you have a fancy, high-tech controllable pitch prop that turns the same direction all the time). This counterclockwise motion when backing causes the stern of the boat to move to port.

You'll know you have prop walk if you try to back out of or into a slip with the rudder centered and you shoot diagonally to the side. To counteract prop walk, you simply compensate for it. Even if you want to back in a straight line, you should turn the wheel to the right before putting the engine in gear. As you back, the right rudder will cancel out the port prop walk and you should back straight if you have enough speed astern. (At very slow speeds, the rudder has minimal effect while backing.)

I say "should" because many boats have a mind of their own when it comes to backing. In case yours does, too, you should always have a back-up plan—no pun intended—when departing a slip. If Plan A is to back to starboard, followed by pulling forward and driving down the fairway, have Plan B in your pocket for when the boat decides to back to port anyway. In Plan B you would simply back all the way out the fairway to open water. There's no shame in this.

Whatever works.

And since we're talking about boats here, and not cars, when both Plan A and B fail to come about, be prepared to come up with a Plan C real fast. Say your boat backs in a straight line this time, bringing your stern right up to the boats across the narrow fairway behind you. What do you do? Simply take a deep breath and calmly back and fill until the bow is pointed where you want to go.

Prop walk isn't always a bad thing. It can work to your advantage when docking port side to a pier. I love portside landings. You pull alongside the dock and put the engine into reverse to take the way off. As you do so, the prop walk kicks your stern to port, settling the stern right against the pier, exactly where you want it.

Nice.

Whether going into a slip or departing one, watch how your bow and stern move in relation to objects around you, then adjust, adjust, adjust. Coming in too fast? Put her in neutral and drift a little. Still too fast? Put her in reverse and slow it down faster. But don't go crazy. Docking is an art. Control your engines and rudder with a light touch.

Boats don't turn on a dime, so if getting into your slip requires a 90-degree turn, you'll have to experiment and find out how early you have to start your turn. It may be quite a bit earlier than you'd think. You don't want to wait until you're at the slip next to yours to start coming left or right. Do that, and you'll likely end up too far down the fairway. Start your turn early, watch your bow in relation to the entrance to your slip, then adjust.

Wind grabbed you? Adjust. Currents pushing you faster than you expected? Reverse. But make your movements calmly and easily. Talk to yourself. Take deep breaths. Resist the urge to turn over the helm to someone else. Guys don't take that luxury. Back out and start over if you have to. You'll learn something every time you dock. Every boat handles differently. The only way to know how yours reacts is to drive it so often that you can predict what moves you have to make for every given situation.

If you have a choice of what slip you'll take or what time you leave and return, do it so that you're maneuvering into the wind and current. This goes back to the fact that you have more control when water is flowing over your rudder. When you maneuver against resistance, your rudder bites in and responds well. If you back or pull forward with the current or wind, you're at their mercy.

As with everything you do on a boat, set yourself up for success so you end up with a positive attitude about docking. You want your first experiences to be easy. After you start to get a real feel for how your boat responds, only then should you move up to more challenging situations.

When you first start practicing:

- Choose a day and time when as few people as possible will be hanging around the marina. You don't need the distraction of Looky-Lous when you're learning.

- Wait for a day with little to no wind. You'll work up to windier days. For now, keep it light.
- Consult your tide table and don't start your practice session until it's slack water. Just as with wind, you'll work up to docking in currents.
- Hang every fender you own over the sides. Borrow some from neighboring boats if that puts you more at ease. Don't be embarrassed by using lots of fenders; that's what they're made for—to protect your boat.

This docking practice will undoubtedly be some of the most valuable time you invest in becoming a better boater. I guarantee you'll be better trained than 99 percent of your fellow boaters who never invest in dedicated docking drills. They may spend hours on the water, but only dock once each time they go out.

The Naval Academy understands the importance of docking practice. They teach future officers to dock ships by doing what they call "bumper drills" with their 95-foot Yard Patrol craft. The midshipmen land these fiberglass boats—small ships, really—alongside the Academy's harbor wall over and over and over. Those YPs are pretty battle scarred, but the staff expects some dings.

You won't ding your boat if you use plenty of fenders, so get out there and practice, practice, practice. Learn how to handle the different kinds of docking scenarios. Start with the easiest kind: landing against a T-head, or the open face of a long pier. Come in starboard-side-to, then turn around and land port-side-to. Then do it again. Try landing between two other boats along the same pier, like parallel parking.

Don't worry about securing the dock lines each time. Make what pilots call "touch and go" landings. Gently kiss the pier with your fenders, then pull right out. That way you get to practice a "landing" and "take-off" all at once . . . a two-fer.

Once you're comfortable with flat-face landings, move up to docking in a slip. Challenge yourself. Notice the difference it makes when you use varying amounts of speed. When landing a boat, a little speed can be good, especially if the wind's really blowing. Be bold and drive with confidence.

If you go to the trouble of learning how to dock well, you'll want to keep your skills sharp. The only way to do this is to keep doing it. I recommend you work out a deal with your partner where you share the docking fifty-fifty. Whoever takes the boat out, brings her in while the other secures the lines. The next time you get under way, switch roles. This way your partner's line handling skills will never get rusty, either.

Remember we talked about a woman's need to "look good?" Believe me, when it comes to docking, guys want to look good, too. It's almost as if there's a silent competition among them. Just like anchoring, male boaters will always watch to see how the other guy does. It's as if they're keeping score.

We used to keep our boat at Herrington Harbor Marina south of Annapolis. The folks on our pier were a pretty rowdy bunch. There was never a shortage of laughs on I-dock. It seemed as if there were a party aboard a different boat nearly every weekend when folks came back in from a day on the water.

One particular Saturday Ty and I were enjoying a get-together on a large motor yacht at the end of the pier. Suddenly the crowd rushed off the boat. Not knowing what was happening, we followed the little parade until it stopped by the empty slip of Marty, one of the more popular guys on the dock. We didn't have long to wonder what was up before Marty's Grand Banks 36 appeared at the end of the fairway and headed toward us.

As soon as they spotted him, the crowd began heckling, yelling out all sorts of "encouraging" docking advice as he turned into his slip:

"A little more to the left, Marty."

"Think you're going a little fast there, Bud."

"Who taught you how to drive a boat? John Deere?"

"Time to call Sea Tow."

In spite of the audience, red-faced Marty did a fine job. He shut down his engine and no doubt breathed a sigh of relief. But the crowd wasn't finished with him yet. A dozen of his fellow boaters pulled out poster-sized placards like the ones judges use at the Olympics, and raised them over their head.

Poor Marty had only scored a 6.5.

It's a fact of docking that yes, people will watch—especially when there's a woman at the helm. They'll watch with great interest to see how you do, but also with a good deal of admiration—men and women alike. They may not hold up score cards, but I guarantee you'll score big points just by taking the helm and making the effort.

15

ANCHORING AND MOORING

You may think that anchoring is nothing more than plopping some heavy metal on the harbor floor before settling down to some smooth jazz and a glass of wine in the cockpit. You drop the hook and forget it. But you're wrong.

Anchoring is a spectator sport. And you're the entertainment.

One of the main reasons boaters watch each other anchor is to watch the antics between husband and wife. These can be so amusing that cruising musician Eileen Quinn has written a song about it. It's one of her most popular tunes because so many boaters have been there and done that.

The problem for couples arises because the anchor is at the bow and the helm is not. Discussions about when and where to let the anchor go and how much chain to let out are nearly impossible to conduct in a conversational tone of voice on larger boats with that much physical separation. Consequently, voices rise. Sound travels extremely well across water, and soon everyone in the anchorage has heard a couple shouting at each other before they've even met them.

One couple who anchored ahead of us in Vero Beach had a unique system to eliminate this problem. The woman took her place at the bow while the man stood at the helm. Being on the flying bridge of a relatively short boat, he could have easily talked to her at not much louder than a normal voice level. I waited to see how they'd do.

Yes, I was watching. About half a dozen of us were watching, because he'd chosen a spot that was a little too close to four boats, including ours. Even though he was near his partner, this guy pulled a whistle out of his pocket and blew it at her. As if she were a dog! He blew a series of annoying tweets that must have meant something to the woman, because she dutifully responded.

It was way too Pavlovian for me.

All I could think was that nobody other than a swim coach had better blow a whistle at me like that. From the look of shock exhibited by the other women in the anchorage, I could tell I wasn't the only one who felt that way. Some of the men, however, appeared to be taking notes.

A clever entrepreneur has solved the shouting problem by marketing a set of radio headsets appropriately known as "Marriage Savers." Couples who use them swear by them. Personally, I prefer the cost-free method: hand signals.

Any gestures that you and your partner agree upon will do the job. Those involving the middle finger are to be avoided, as they defeat the purpose. Ty and I have a series of signals that work for us:

- "Come ahead easy": one (index) finger up, pointing in the direction to maneuver.
- "Back easy": one finger pointed straight down.
- "Back a little harder": two fingers pointed straight down.
- "Engine in neutral": a closed fist.
- "Anchor's up/maneuver at will": one finger twirling in the air.
- "Anchor's set/kill the engine": the throat-cut sign.

These are the only signals we ever need. When the person at the bow gives a signal, the person at the helm mirrors it back to confirm they saw it.

Couples who use hand signals disappoint audiences expecting fireworks. Once you get your routine down, you'll provide entertainment of a different sort: a beautifully choreographed dance, completely silent and synchronized.

The other reason boaters watch each other anchor is to make sure they do it right. Anchors know Murphy's Law. If they're going to drag, they usually wait until their owners are either asleep or not on board. It's bad enough to wonder if your own anchor's set well. It's worse yet to watch someone who doesn't know what they're doing set the hook badly directly ahead of you. And those guys are out there.

We were enjoying cocktails in our cruising buddies' cockpit in Ibiza when a 40-foot catamaran sailed in and dropped the hook just forward of our two boats. Ibiza is a happening place, and within five minutes of arriving, everyone aboard the cat zipped off in their dinghy, no doubt anxious to discover what was happening ashore.

Half an hour later, the four of us on *Concerto* all noticed the catamaran at the same time. It was drifting sideways between our two boats at a pretty good clip, heading straight for another anchored vessel. While my friend June and I alerted this boat's crew to the fact that they were about to have an unwanted visitor pinned against their bow, Ty and Geoff jumped in our dinghy. Within seconds they were aboard the errant cat.

It's always good practice to leave the key in the ignition for just such a crisis. Luckily, the owners had done so. Our two heroes started the engines and steered the boat away from the other just in time. What they thought would be a simple matter of re-setting the anchor, however, turned into a 45-minute drill. Why? Because that big catamaran only had a 22-pound anchor—totally inadequate for a boat of that size.

Over and over the guys dropped that silly little anchor. When they finally got it to hold, it was in a spot a full half-mile from where the owners had left it. We waited a while for them to come back, but these fellows must have been serious partiers. We finally went to bed, and all I could think about was the surprise that awaited them when they got back and discovered their boat was gone.[13]

So boat owners have good reason for wanting to make sure those around them have set their anchors well, using an appropriately sized anchor and the proper length of chain or rope. Nevertheless, it's one thing to casually glance over at new arrivals and make sure they know what they're doing. The ones who really annoy me are the guys who see you coming and walk up to the bow and stand there with their Mr. Clean pose: legs planted shoulder-width apart, arms crossed firmly across the chest, and deadly serious expressions on their faces.

Give me a chance, guys. I don't want their hull paint on my boat any more than they want mine on theirs.

Don't give others a reason to worry. Show them you know what you're doing. Anchoring is not difficult. It's a matter of learning the basics and applying them. Doing it well comes down to making good choices: Will you drop the hook or pick up a mooring? Where's the best spot? How heavy an anchor do you need? Should you use line or chain? How much line or chain should you let out? How do you make sure the anchor digs in?

Mooring vs. Anchoring

A mooring is a heavy object, placed on the bottom, which is attached to a float on the surface by either line or chain. The weight is usually a large concrete block, although it can be an actual anchor, a mechanically set screw, or even an old engine. Whatever the weight, it's much heavier than any anchor you'd carry on your boat.

Most floats already have a mooring line attached. To use a mooring, you approach slowly, stopping when your bow is directly beside

[13] As we sailed out of the harbor the next morning, we saw that the catamaran's dinghy was tied astern. Obviously, they'd found it.

the float. Try to approach upwind of the float so your bow will drift toward it instead of away, and grab the mooring line with your boat hook. You cleat the mooring line to one of your bow cleats, and voilá, you're moored.

When it's time to leave, you simply drop the mooring line in the water (unless you've used your own line) and head out, taking care not to run over the line with your propeller.

Moorings are either private, set by their owners for their own boats, or they're available for public use, set by individuals, marinas, or communities in popular coves and harbors. They are deliberately placed so boats won't swing into each other. Some public moorings are free, but they have a time limit for their use, such as 24 or 48 hours. Most come with a use fee.

In spite of the fee, many boaters prefer mooring over anchoring because it's easier. The problem with moorings is that you don't know what's under the float. How heavy is the weight? How strong is the line between the float and the weight, and what is its condition?

Anchoring may take a little longer than picking up a mooring, but you always know what's holding you to the bottom and what kind of shape your equipment's in.

If you boat in New England, you're well familiar with moorings, because they're everywhere, and can be quite expensive. Some of the most popular coves in Maine are completely filled with bobbing floats, leaving nowhere to drop an anchor, even if you wanted to.

Other parts of the country haven't caught the mooring craze, however. In that case, you have no choice but to anchor.

Location, Location, Location

Where you drop your hook is a critical decision. It can mean the difference between setting your anchor well or dragging onto rocks, between sleeping well or rocking from side to side all night. Many charts will show an anchor symbol in places that are particularly well suited to anchoring. Cruising guides will also recommend good spots to drop the hook. This doesn't mean these are the only places to anchor. Sometimes it's fun to find a spot that nobody else knows about, away from other boats, if you so choose.

Select your location based on the following:

• Shelter – A sheltered anchorage is one that is protected from both wind and waves. While it's nice to find a round cove with land on three sides, these aren't always available. Ideally, look for a spot that will put a piece of land or a jetty between you and the wind. Obviously, the wind changes direction, so what may be a protected spot one day, may be a poor choice the next. There's nothing wrong with spending the night off an open beach if the wind is coming from the shore. The worst situation is to anchor with the wind blowing you toward the shore or a wall. Should your anchor drag, you'll blow right onto the lee shore.

• Type of bottom. Symbols on the chart or in cruising guides will describe the bottom at the place you're considering. You want something that your anchor will dig into, such as sand, clay, grass, or sticky mud. In general, soft is better than hard, but soft mud may not provide enough friction. Sand is the best. Avoid rock and never anchor in coral.

• Depth. Choose a spot that will leave, at the very least, one foot of water under your boat at low tide. Even with that amount, if there's any kind of wave action, you may bounce on the bottom. Realistically, you should have three feet under the keel as a minimum. To make sure there will be enough water throughout an entire tide cycle, add the height of the lowest tide shown on your tide table to the soundings on your chart. Make sure that if your boat were to swing in a complete circle, there'd be plenty of good water throughout, not just where you are at the time you drop the anchor.

• Swing room. One of the neatest places we've ever anchored was at the base of Chatterbox Falls in British Columbia. The bow of our boat was right where the roaring water emptied into Princess Louisa Inlet. It was noisy, but beautiful. Because of the constant flow from the waterfall, our boat stayed facing the same direction during our entire visit. This is unusual. Be aware when you choose the spot to anchor that as the wind or current changes, your boat may swing through every degree of the compass during the time you're there. This is called your swing circle. The diameter of this circle will be twice as long as your anchor rode, so it's important to know how much line or chain you put out and exactly where your anchor is. If there are boats around you, they'll most likely swing with you, but not always. Others may have more or less rode out than you do, so leave plenty of room.

Ground Tackle

I have yet to sit down with other cruising couples when the guys don't start discussing anchors. I don't know what it is, but men are really concerned about size. They just love to compare their equipment.

As a female boater, you may not find it the most scintillating topic, but you should at least know how to choose the right anchoring equipment, known as ground tackle. This term applies to anchors, rode, and all the shackles and other gear used to connect the two.

• Anchors. While the weight of any anchor is important for its holding power, how well it digs into the bottom is equally important. Anchors come in many designs, some better suited than others for various bottom types. Most powerboats and lighter sailboats carry a steel anchor known as a Danforth. This is the kind with two pointy flukes.

Cruising sailboats, being heavier and anchoring in more demanding areas, usually carry heavier anchors designed for use with a variety of bottom types. Most marine stores or catalogues include charts showing the different types of anchors and what kind of bottom they're best suited for, along with the recommended weight for a particular boat length. A good rule of thumb for coastal boating is one pound of weight for one foot of boat length. Cruising boats usually go up to the next size larger anchor. When in doubt, heavier is better.

• Rode. Most boats under 30 feet usually anchor with a rode consisting of line attached to a short length of chain. Larger vessels and almost all cruising boats use all-chain rode. Line is cheaper, lighter, and springier than chain, but chain has several significant advantages over line: the additional weight adds to the total weight of the ground tackle. Chain is heavy, so it lies along the bottom for a good distance back from the anchor. This helps prevent the anchor from pulling up and out. Chain is resistant to chafe and won't cut on coral or rocks as line will. Chain stows easily, with gravity doing most of the work, whereas line must be hand-coiled.

Setting an Anchor

Once you've chosen the perfect spot and have the proper equipment for your boat, you're ready to anchor. The actual process is quite easy:

• Bring the bow of the boat into the wind.

This is very important because this is the way your boat will naturally lie after the anchor is set. Also, you're going to bring your boat to a complete stop before dropping the anchor and backing down (explanation follows). If you're facing into the wind, the wind will help you to stop, then push you backward in the direction you want to back. If you anchor downwind, you may override your own anchor line and get it tangled in your prop.

This happened to a boat that was anchoring within view of our table at an Annapolis restaurant one afternoon. Ty had obviously been more intent on watching the couple anchor than on listening to the conversation between our server and me, because he burst out, "Look at those fools anchoring downwind." I interrupted him before he could put his foot any deeper in his mouth and said, "Yes, honey, those are our server's parents."

Oops.

If there are other boats in the anchorage, simply observe how they're lying and approach your spot heading the same way.

• Stop the boat. Remember to first move forward of the spot where you want the boat to lie when it's at the end of the rode, because you're going to drift back after you drop the anchor. Make sure you've come to a complete stop by watching your motion in relation to immobile objects ashore or on the water.

• Let go the anchor. Initially only let out enough rode for the anchor to reach the bottom with a little slack in the rode.

• Determine the amount of scope required and start letting it out. Scope is the ratio of the length of anchor rode to the vertical distance from the bow of your boat to the bottom of the water. Under normal conditions, if anchoring on chain, 4:1 or 5:1 is a good average. If on nylon line or using a lightweight anchor, 6:1 or 7:1 is good. If heavy winds are predicted, use a higher ratio up to 10:1.

Here's how this works: If you're in six feet of water at high tide (don't forget to factor in the tide) and your bow is four feet off the water, that's a vertical distance of ten feet from the bottom of the water to your bow. If you're anchoring in normal conditions on chain and want a scope of 5:1, that would be five times ten, or a rode length of fifty feet.

Using the proper amount of scope ensures that the pull of the rode on your anchor parallels the bottom as closely as possible. If there's not enough scope, the angle of the rode from your bow to the anchor may be such that it pulls the flukes right out.

• Start backing slowly if the wind doesn't push you on its own. Do this while the rode is still paying out so it doesn't all end up in a big pile on the bottom.

• Shift into neutral and let the boat drift back on the anchor.

• Help the anchor to set by backing slowly again. You should be able to tell if your anchor has set by resting your hand on the rode. It will go taut when the anchor digs in. If you back too quickly, it will jerk the anchor across the bottom, never allowing it to set properly. If your boat didn't back in a straight line, you'll really feel it when the line goes taut and your boat swings back in line all by itself. Smile when that happens, because you know your anchor has set.

• Back just a little harder. This simply sets the anchor better.

• Take bearings to objects ashore. Choose two objects at different angles from your boat and notice where they are in relation to where you settle. Watch for several minutes to make sure you're not dragging. Of course, if the wind changes direction and you swing, your bearings to these objects will change.

Now that you know how to anchor correctly, you'll understand why we were so amused by a couple we watched anchor one evening in the San Juan Islands off the coast of Washington. We were the only ones in the anchorage until this young man and woman motored in on a trawler. He went to the bow while she took the helm. She stopped the boat and he dropped a little Fortress anchor into the water.

The water in the cove was about ten feet deep. We watched him let out no more than fifteen feet of line, then cleat it off. We looked at each other incredulously. The rode was practically vertical.

Next he told the woman to back the boat, and she did exactly that...going about ten knots. I could just see that little anchor skipping merrily along the bottom as the trawler went full speed astern.

The poor kids repeated this process over and over until Ty flagged them down.

"Having a little trouble?" he asked.

The guy shook his head. "Yeah, I don't know what the problem is. This is my dad's boat, and he never has trouble getting the anchor to set."

Need I say more? Ground tackle is important, but so is technique. Remember: Come to a complete stop into the wind. Let go the anchor and let out enough scope. Back down easy, then back just a little harder. Now you can see why the hand signals mentioned previously are all you need.

If you're going to be doing the anchoring aboard your vessel and want to get into more details, I highly recommend *The Complete Book of Anchoring and Mooring* by Earl Hinz. In my opinion, this book gives by far the most thorough coverage of the subject.

Preventing Disaster

Even the best-set anchor can break loose. Don't just set your anchor and forget it. Keep an eye on things.

But you have to sleep sometime, right? The best way to get a good night's sleep while at anchor is to set an anchor drag alarm. Most marine GPS units and some chart plotters come with one. Once your anchor is set, you set the alarm and indicate how far you're willing to let the boat move before the alarm goes off.

Once the alarm is turned on, if your boat moves outside the parameters you've set, you'll know it. We usually set our alarm for .03 nautical miles, which is 180 feet. In a tight anchorage, we'll set it at .02, or 120 feet. This allows the boat to swing normally through its swing circle without the alarm constantly sounding.

That little bit of insurance saved our boat. We had picked up a mooring at Little Farmers Cay in the Exumas. We normally prefer to anchor, but our buddy boat was on a mooring, so we followed suit.

Bad decision.

At 11:30 that night, the anchor drag alarm went off, waking us from a sound sleep. Yes, we'd set the alarm, even though we were on a mooring, because you can never be too safe. It turned out to be a good move. The mooring pendant had parted below the water and we were rapidly drifting backwards. Ty ran forward and immediately dropped the anchor while I went to the wheel, just in case we needed to maneuver. Once we were stopped, we took a look at the chart.

If it hadn't been for the anchor alarm, we would have drifted right onto a coral reef. Luckily we were alerted in time and the boat survived to see many other anchorages.

Your boat is a big investment. Good ground tackle and drag alarms are your best insurance. Carry the proper equipment for your boat and learn how to use it correctly. As you can see, there's not much to it. You need only apply a few basic rules and cautions to ensure a good night's sleep for yourself and those around you.

16

SAILING

A good-natured rivalry exists between sailors and power boaters. To the one with sails, the other is a "stinkpot," those boats that tear around making all that noise and throwing out the big wake. ("But gee, it must be nice to zip over to The Crab Claw in time for lunch, when it takes us two days to get there.")

To the one with the big engines, the other is a "blow-boat," an obstacle in the channel that keeps claiming the right of way. ("But wouldn't it be great not to have to pay for all this fuel?")

Some boaters make the switch from one type of vessel to the other, but for the most part, you either crave the canvas or feel the need for speed. If you fit into the latter category, you're welcome to skip this chapter, but maybe you'll stick around and find out how the other half lives.

For hundreds of years, men have been going to sea in sailing ships. It's about time women do the same. Sailboats may require greater physical effort than powerboats. They may expose you more to the elements. But it's nothing a woman can't manage. Winches make the lines easier to handle and foul-weather gear keeps you dry. So if your attitude's properly adjusted and the sails sing to your soul, the challenge of harnessing the wind is yours for the taking.

Most sailboats over 20 feet have an engine, whether it be a small outboard motor or an 85-horsepower inboard diesel. So technically, if your boat has a propeller, you don't ever have to bother to sail. You could be out there tooling around on the water the day you buy your boat and only need to learn how she handles.

That seems a little ridiculous, doesn't it? I mean, who would own a sailboat and not know how to sail? Well, let me tell you . . . .

We were anchored at Cambridge Cay in the Bahamas. Our friends Skip and Cathy had joined us for dinner aboard, and we were discussing the day's sail. Skip asked if we'd listened to the distress call on channel 16. We must have been out of range, because we hadn't heard a thing.

He told us that two women were having engine trouble with their sailboat. From what he could gather, the two ladies didn't know how to sail. They were adrift in deep water, far from the protection of the shallow Bahama banks.

We shook our heads, confused. Skip must have heard wrong. If the women had a boat big enough to have an engine, it wasn't just a local day-sailer. Why didn't they just raise their sails and head for an anchorage? With no other information, we shrugged our shoulders and moved on to other subjects.

One week later, Ty and I were at the Nassau Harbor Club. We had just finished making a phone call to family and were turning to leave the marina office, when two women walked by.

The smaller of the two looked at us and said, "You can't possibly be sailors; you're smiling too much."

Her odd comment caught me off guard. "Sounds like you've had a bad experience."

"Oh, you might say that," her partner said, rolling her eyes.

Recalling the previous week's conversation with Skip and Cathy, a little light bulb turned on. "You wouldn't happen to be the two women who got in some trouble off Cambridge Cay last week, would you?"

"That would be us," she replied, and proceeded to fill us in on the details.

The two had owned powerboats in the past and now thought it might be fun to try sailing. They took a class together and learned the basics, then they went out and bought a boat. A big boat. They found an Irwin 38—no small investment—and threw an additional $50,000 into fixing her up. These weren't just cosmetic improvements, mind you. These ladies did their homework. They installed radar, solar panels, hand rails . . . all kinds of things that serious cruising sailboats have.

They lived in Florida, but dreamed of sailing in the Bahamas. Anxious to get to the islands, but aware of their lack of experience, they hired a captain. From the sound of it, the captain didn't know much more than they did. By the time they got to Nassau, they were disgusted with the guy. Figuring they knew how to read a chart and drive a boat, they sent the captain packing and headed down-island.

Somewhere north of Cambridge Cay their diesel engine started acting up. Then it died completely. They fumbled with their tools, all the while drifting farther out to sea. Yes, but they'd taken sailing lessons, right? All they had to do was sail to the nearest island, drop the hook, and call on the VHF to find someone who could help them with their engine.

The problem was, they'd never raised their sails. Not once.

Maybe I'm missing something, but why take lessons if you're not going to try what you learned aboard your own boat? Why go all the way to the Bahamas on a sailboat you've invested a lot of money in, if you're not going to sail it?

A catamaran with an experienced skipper aboard answered the ladies' call for help on Channel 16. He sailed up beside them and talked them through raising their main and jib. He instructed them how to trim the sails for the course they needed to steer, and accompanied them to a sheltered anchorage.

Once they got their anchor down and set, that was it. They swore off sailing forever. They hired another captain to take them back to Nassau, even though they were under tow the whole way. When we met them they were making arrangements to put the boat up for sale.

What an expensive lesson. Perhaps their lack of initiative in applying what they learned in class had something to do with the fear factor. Yes, sailboats heel when the sails are up. Yes, the sails make a lot of noise when they flap. No, you can't stop a sailboat by putting it in reverse. But none of these are problems when you understand how sails and sailboats work.

Sailing is more involved than motoring, but anyone can learn to do it. Like anything else, first you study the theory, then you apply what you learn with hands-on practice. The more you sail, the better you get at it, and the less intimidating it all seems.

Just as with boating in general, if you're going to be a sailor, you have to speak the language. Most of the terms you learned in the chapter on nautical terminology apply to sailing, but sailboats have a number of parts not found on powerboats. As you'll see, sailors turn a simple thing like a piece of canvas into a linguistic challenge, giving a different name to each of a sail's three sides and each of its three corners.

Yet the precise names allow you to refer to the parts of a sail and related gear immediately, without resorting to pointing and talking about "that thing at the end of the boom." It helps speed things up immensely and shows you know what you're talking about when you can say, "Please attach the outhaul to the clew so we can tighten up the foot of the main."

If that last sentence sounded foreign to you, study the following diagram and memorize the terms before going any further:

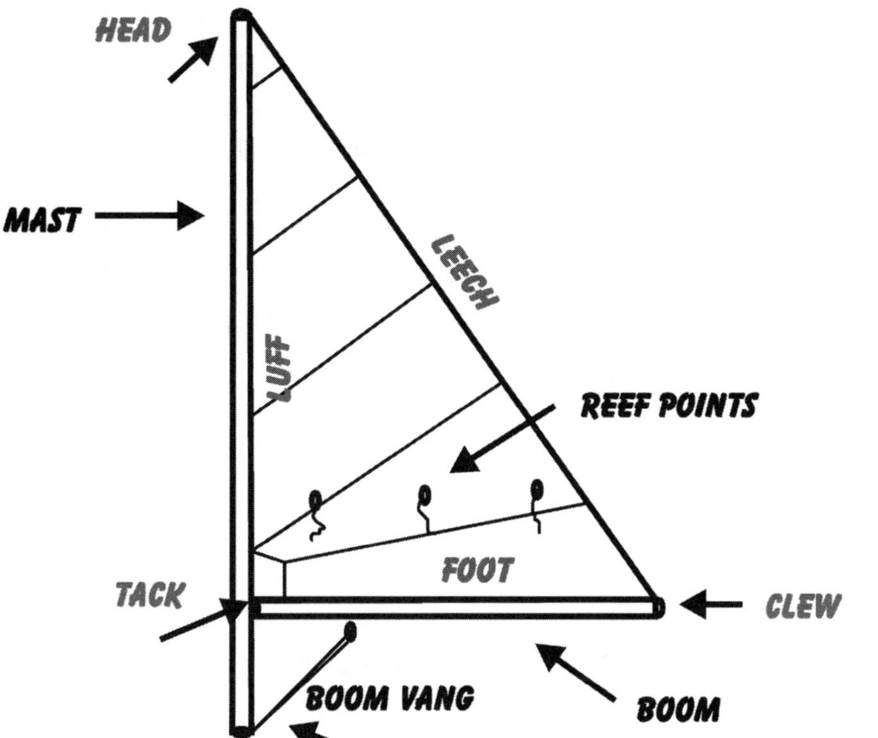

Fig. 16.1

Got all that? Good. You're going to see some of those words again soon.

The first thing most people new to sailing want to know is, "How do those sails work?" I mean, it's obvious when the wind's coming from astern and the sails are out all the way, that the wind is just pushing the boat forward. But lots of sailboats under way have their sails trimmed almost parallel to the boat instead of way out to catch the air. If the wind's blowing across the beam, what keeps the boat from moving sideways?

It's all about physics. Now, if you enjoyed that subject in school even a fraction more than I did, you'll probably like studying about Center of Effort (CE), Center of Lateral Resistance (CLR), lift, drag, vectors, and all the other technical stuff dealing with the physics of sailing that you'll find in any book dedicated solely to the topic.

In all honesty, I do find the science of sailing fascinating, because it deals with a subject near and dear to my heart. But for our purposes here, I'll simplify things.

The hull of a sailboat is designed to act as a hydrofoil. When water flows over the curved surface of the hull it creates higher pressure on one side of the keel than the other, and the keel's foil pulls to windward. The sails, when trimmed just right, act as airfoils, like an airplane wing. When air flows over the curved surface of the sails, it creates higher pressure on the outside of the curve and lower pressure on the inside, and the sails' foils pull to leeward. The opposing forces of the sails and the hull keep the boat moving forward instead of sideways.

Sailing is all a matter of shaping the sails just right in relation to the wind angle to maximize these driving forces. If the wind were always blowing against the sails from the same angle, there'd be nothing to it. You'd raise the sails and set them at the same angle you always do, then off you'd go. But then there'd be no challenge. It would get dull pretty quickly.

Of course, the wind is always changing direction, and so are you, if you want to go anywhere but in a straight line away from your marina. So you need to learn how to set the sails just right, or trim them, for every possible wind angle. You learn this first from a book, and then you get out there on the water and try it.

I have yet to find a book on sailing that doesn't discuss what are called the "points of sail," including a diagram to explain them. Not to be outdone, I hereby introduce you to (drum roll, please):

The Points of Sail

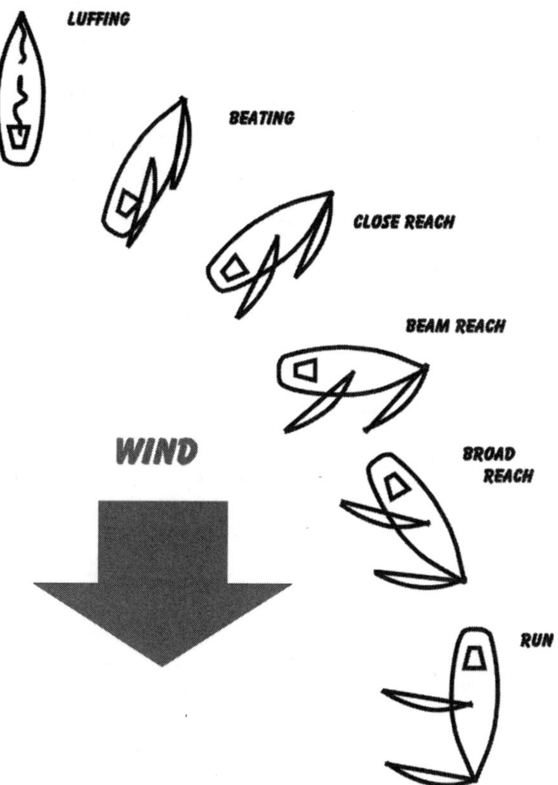

Fig. 16.2

Air must move unequally across the curved surface of a sail to create lift. It flows faster around the convex side and slower along the concave side. Thus you can see why a sailboat can't sail directly into the wind. When the wind is "on the nose," or coming from straight ahead, as it is with the top, left boat in figure 16.2 above, the air flows down both sides of the sails pretty much equally. Without a difference in pressure between one side and the other, the sails just waggle back and forth. This is called luffing. (Notice from figure 16.1 [page 175] that the leading edge of a sail is called the luff.)

Luffing is not always a bad thing. You want the sails to luff when you raise them so there's no pressure on the sails or slide cars as they travel up the mast track or forestay.

To raise the sails, you steer the boat until the bow is directly into the wind. If you have a wind direction arrow at the top of your mast or on a graphical instrument at your helm, steer the boat until the arrow is pointing straight ahead. Lacking these, steer until your flag is flying directly aft and you feel the wind right in your face (hence the term "on the nose").

You want your mainsheet slack at this point. The mainsheet controls the boom. When you raise the mainsail, slacking the mainsheet allows the boom to dance around a bit. As long as you keep the boat headed into the wind, it's not going to go too far and will help keep the main luffing as the sail goes up.[14] If there's a decent breeze blowing, your sail is going to make a lot of flapping noise. The stronger the wind, the more sound and fury from your sails as they luff. Don't let all that racket scare you. Your sails are doing exactly what you want them to do at this point.

If your headsail is not on a roller furler,[15] you'll raise it right after you raise the main, while still headed into the wind. With a roller-furled headsail, you can wait until after you've fallen off to unfurl the sail.[16]

So now it's time to trim your sails. Start steering the boat to the heading you desire, adjusting the mainsheet as you turn. Steady the boat on your course, and following the general guidelines in figure 16.2, trim your sails according to the angle the wind is crossing your deck.

---

[14] Many sailboats now have in-mast or in-boom furling, which allows you to simply unfurl the sail by pulling a line. All the principles discussed here about heading into the wind, luffing, and sail trim apply equally regardless of whether you raise your sails or unfurl them.

[15] A roller furler is a wonderfully convenient device that allows you to wrap your jib around the headstay when not in use. This eliminates the need to hank on the sail each time you use it or to stow it in a bag on deck.

[16] "Falling off" means to head away from the wind.

For example, if the wind is crossing your deck directly over the port or starboard beam, you trim for a beam reach. As you see in the diagram, on a beam reach the boom is out about 45 degrees, so trim your mainsheet accordingly. Then adjust your jib sheets so the air flows just right across the jib. You want to create a nice slot between both sails.

The more you study the subject, the more you'll learn all the nifty sail trimming tricks, such as watching the telltales, those little pieces of yarn or ribbons attached to sails that allow you to actually see the air flow.

From there it's all about making adjustments. You tweak your sails, letting them out, then pulling them in, maybe a little and maybe a lot, watching the effect every little change you make has on your speed. You observe how other boats going the same way as you are have their sails trimmed, and if everyone on the water seems to be going faster than you, you figure out what you need to do differently.

One September Sunday we were sailing home from St. Michael's on the eastern shore of Chesapeake Bay. We were heading west on the Tred Avon River with an easterly wind pushing us along on a great downwind run. A mile ahead of us, we noticed a sailboat about the same length as ours going in the same direction we were.

At first I thought they were under power because both their main and jib were trimmed in almost to the centerline, instead of let way out to catch the wind. It became clear as we rapidly overtook them that they were actually sailing. Well, I don't know if you could call it sailing, when they were just kind of drifting along.

We passed them so quickly that it was almost embarrassing. We were close enough to say hello, but I knew it wasn't my place to tell them they'd go a lot faster if they would let their sails out. I hoped they'd notice the drastic difference between our sail trim and theirs, and adjust accordingly.

We kept stealing surreptitious glances astern after we passed, but for five minutes nothing happened. Then we saw both sails billow outward like a blossoming flower. By George, they'd gotten it. Needless to say, once they had their sails properly set, their speed increased immediately.

Funny how that works.

Now, if a sailboat can't sail into the wind because it loses the air-foil effect, what do you do when you want to travel on a course where the wind will be directly on the nose?

You turn on the engine.

Just kidding. While that's certainly an option if you're in a hurry to get somewhere, once you start the engine, you're just a power vessel. Real sailboats tack.

Tacking involves altering your course at an angle to your desired track until the wind is far enough off the bow that you're able to sail. Depending on their design, some boats can sail closer to the wind than others before stalling.

When you can't sail in the direction you want to go because the wind's dead ahead, you fall off and trim the sails until the boat moves forward and you're happy with your speed. When you've sailed as far off your intended track as you care to go, it's time to tack. Steer the bow of the boat toward the wind, just as when you bring it into the wind to raise or lower the sails. But don't stop there. Keep going past the point where the wind's on the nose and fall off onto the other tack.

Say you're close-hauled on a starboard tack.[17] The wind is crossing your deck about 45 degrees off your starboard bow. To tack the boat, you turn toward the wind (in this case, to starboard). You steer the bow of the boat through the wind until the wind is coming across the port side at the same angle as it was when you were on a starboard tack—45 degrees. You're now close-hauled on a port tack, and you trim your sails accordingly.

When you get as far off your intended track as you care to go on

---

17 As discussed in the chapter on "Rules of the Road" for sailing vessels, starboard tack is when the wind is blowing across the starboard side of the boat and the sails are out to port. Port tack is when the wind is blowing across the port side of the boat and the sails are out to starboard.

this new tack, you simply tack back the other way. And so on and so forth. Tacking is nothing more than turning the boat by bringing the bow of the boat through the wind. If you're only going a short distance, your tacks will be shorter than if you have a long way to travel.

You can see that tacking can add miles to your track, but that's all part of sailing. Tacking the boat on a day with good winds can be exhilarating as you swing the bow through the wind, release the jib sheet from one side, and sheet it in on the other. It's great fun to challenge yourself to see how quickly you can trim the sails without losing speed.

This is the perfect time to discuss one of the things that often frightens women who are new to sailing: the feeling that they have no control over a boat under sail. If you want to stop a powerboat, you simply put the engine in reverse. But how do you stop a sailboat that's being propelled along by the wind? Easy. You do a "quick stop maneuver" and back (or backwind) the jib.

To back the jib, simply tack the boat, but don't release the jib sheet. In other words, turn the wheel and bring the bow of the boat through the wind, but leave the jib sheet on the winch. As you go through the wind, the jib will flop over to the opposite side, but because the sheet is still attached, the wind will fill in behind the sail.

If you were sailing under jib alone, the boat would now come to an almost complete stop. Under normal circumstances, however, the mainsail will also be raised. To take the strain off the main, simply ease the mainsheet all the way out. The boom will fall in line with the wind and the main will luff. This procedure of backing the jib and slacking the main is called heaving-to. It's a magical way of bringing the boat to a near stop no matter how strong the winds are. I say "near stop" because the boat may creep along at about one knot or so. You'll need to play with the wheel on your boat to find out where to set the rudder to slow your boat as much as possible.

You will want to stop your boat immediately if something or

someone falls overboard. For this reason, you should always be conscious of where the wind is coming from. This sounds obvious, but to a new sailor, it takes a while for wind sense to become second nature. Until it does, as you sail along, ask yourself, "Which side of the boat is the wind crossing? Which way would I turn if I had to stop the boat, or tack, right now?" This should become so automatic that if someone fell in the water, your first reaction would be to steer the bow through the wind and backwind the jib.

Another way to stop the boat is to simply come up into the wind. Be aware that this won't immediately halt your forward progress, so don't use this method in an emergency. You'll continue to drift for a short distance, but the sails will be luffing, so they won't be driving you anymore.

As you can see, there should never be a reason for you to feel out of control on a sailboat. We discussed fear of heeling in the chapter on fear. Now's a good time to go back and review that section if this is still an issue for you. Even though you know that your boat's not going to tip over, don't be embarrassed if you don't like to heel excessively. We all have different levels of comfort. For some, 15 degrees is the limit. Others can handle a 25-degree heel or more with no problem.

If the wind picks up and the boat's heeling more than you'd like, simply ease the sheets a bit. In a big gust, ease the mainsheet a lot, then trim it again once the gust is over. This is called depowering the sails. If the wind continues to blow so much that your sails are overpowered, the solution is to reef your sails.

Reefing is nothing more than reducing the total area of one or more of your sails. You'll usually start with your main. Different boats have different systems of reefing, but the principle is the same on all: you bring the boat into the wind to take the pressure off the sail, then you either lower or furl the main until it's a smaller triangle than it was before. You'll have to ensure that the main is securely lashed or furled at the boom and that the halyard is good and tight when you're finished. When all is set, fall off, trim the sail, and continue on your previous course.

When's the best time to reef? Remember this rule: The first time you think about it. As soon as anyone on the boat asks, "Do you think we should reef?" the answer should always be yes. Why? Because the longer you wait, the more likely it is that the wind will continue to increase. The stronger the wind blows, the harder it is to handle the sails.

Reefing takes a little practice. Don't wait until you actually need to reef to try it for the first time. Reef your sails several times in light winds until you can do it quickly and safely. Practice taking one reef, then shaking it out. Next put in a double reef, then a third, if your sail is rigged for three reefs. The next time you're sailing and the wind pipes up, you'll be glad you took the time to practice.

In the chapter on weather, I told you my story about the incident with the squall when I was on the Naval Academy sloop. Our sails weren't reefed because we hadn't been expecting high winds. At the time, we were running with the wind astern. The boom was way out to starboard. When the squall hit and the wind suddenly veered, it grabbed the boom and slammed it over to the port side. This is called an accidental jibe because we were neither expecting it nor prepared for it.

Jibing is not necessarily a bad thing. In fact, when executed correctly, it's as normal and seamanlike a maneuver as tacking. While tacking is bringing the bow of the boat through the wind to make good a desired course, jibing is bringing the stern of the boat through the wind to steer a desired course.

If you're sailing downwind and you want to come to a course that will put the wind on the other side of the boom, you can always steer all the way around and tack, but that requires going in almost a full circle. That doesn't make sense. Instead, do a controlled jibe.

Slowly start turning toward your new course. As the stern comes about, pull in your mainsheet. As the wind passes a point just over

180 degrees astern of you, the boom will cross the boat's centerline and flop over to the other side. That's a jibe. Now you simply ease the mainsheet as you continue on to your desired course until your main is out at an appropriate angle. At this point the jib will be back-winded, so release it from the winch and quickly winch it in on the new tack. If there are enough hands on board, some can handle the jib while others take care of the mainsheet.

Because you've been taking in the mainsheet as you turn, the boom is almost centerlined when the boat jibes. It doesn't have far to go and isn't going to slam over. It's all very controlled and safe, just like the name of this maneuver with which you should be very familiar.

Uncontrolled jibes can happen any time you're sailing downwind. You can lose your attention while steering or the wind can shift just enough to throw the boom over. Whatever the cause, because the boom is out so far when on a run, it has a long way to slam. Unintentional jibes put a lot of stress on your gear and can be extremely dangerous if your boom height is at human level.

Whenever you're on a downwind run, rig a preventer. This can be either a block and tackle assembly made just for this purpose, or a simple line attached to a bail on the boom that is then led to a cleat. Should you jibe with a preventer rigged, the boom will only travel as far as the preventer allows. It's good insurance.

Tacking, jibing, heaving-to, reefing . . . learn these skills and practice them until you're comfortable with them. Don't be like the two women who had a beautiful boat but never raised their sails. What may seem intimidating at first, will soon be effortless and fun.

Sailing can be addictive. It's exhilarating one moment and blissfully peaceful the next. Once you know how to control your sails, you can travel wherever the wind blows, be it that quiet little cove just around the point, or an exotic, far-off land.

It's a feeling of freedom unmatched on land.

17

ENGINES

I feel safe in saying that most women are more than willing to leave engine repair and maintenance to their partner, as I am. I don't know if it's hormonal or the way we're raised, but even though I'm happy to have an engine on my boat, I don't care to get up-close and personal with it.

That having been said, it pays to be familiar with every piece of equipment on your boat, and few are as important as your engine. When it comes to this vital piece of machinery, what you don't know may not hurt you, but it could easily hurt your engine. Neglect certain easy yet critical checks, and you could end up facing some expensive repairs.

Having two X chromosomes and being married to a former ship's engineer, I have little motivation to assume primary care of our boat's engine. I do, however, know enough to perform basic checks and to add my two cents' worth. I'm especially good at this when things go wrong, as they did on *Liberty*'s maiden voyage.

It was a few minutes past midnight. With light winds and a schedule to meet, we were moving ahead under both sail and engine. I had just gotten off watch and snuggled into the pilot berth. I'd barely closed my eyes when suddenly the engine sputtered to a stop.

Lifting my head from the pillow, I waited for the predictable four words from Ty. He didn't disappoint me as he jumped up from the nav table, stuck his head through the companionway, and asked our crew member anxiously, "Did you do that?"

A negative reply propelled Ty into action, barking commands to grab the toolbox and flashlight. In the glow of the red lights, I could almost see his mind working, running through the possible causes of the malfunction. As I unhooked the lee cloth and reluctantly abandoned my warm bunk, Ty peered into the engine room, shining a light on the despicable troublemaker.

Why was he going to General Quarters, I wondered? Even though Ty knew all about diesel engines, I had a feeling the solution was fairly simple, and voiced my inexpert opinion out loud: "I'll bet we're out of fuel in the big tank."

Ty didn't even bother to look up. "No way. The main tank holds 90 gallons. There should be plenty left."

Theoretically, he was right. We'd been told the boat would burn one gallon of diesel per hour, and we hadn't motored more than 45 hours so far. But maybe the previous owner was wrong. After all, to him the boat was little more than a floating condo. He'd rarely left the pier.

"Why don't we just check the tank?" I suggested.

The clatter of wrenches as Ty rummaged through the toolbox was deafening.

Hesitant to question a man who'd spent years in an engine room, I tried a different tack. "You're the one who always tells me to check the most obvious solution first. So I think we may have run out of fuel."

Unable to ignore his own wise teaching, Ty stood up from the engine and huffed his way to the tank.

The dipstick came out like a dry twig.

Wise enough to keep any smart comments to myself, I thanked God that the problem was easily fixed, and opened the valve on the reserve tank. Unfortunately, Ty had to bleed off the air that had been sucked into the fuel lines when the main tank ran dry, but we were soon back under way. My suggestion to check the simplest solution first had saved us time and frustration.

Engines are pretty simple once you get to know them. If you want to know how yours works in detail, there are several books on the market that make the subject easy to understand. My favorite is *Know Your Boat* by David Kroenke.

You don't have to be mechanically inclined to participate in the basics of your engine's upkeep. Look at the problem we had on *Liberty*'s maiden voyage. It didn't take much mechanical ability to figure out we'd run out of fuel. If you want to get a little more involved and do things like changing filters, ask your partner or a friend who knows engines, or hire a mechanic to teach you how.

For an engine to continue operating well, whether inboard or outboard, gasoline or diesel powered, it needs four things:

- Clean fuel
- Clean oil
- Cooling water
- Air

You don't have to understand injection pumps, carburetors, cam shafts, pistons, or transmissions unless you want to. Simply provide your engine with these four components and it should keep on ticking. Have an understanding of why they're important, and you may be able to fix problems yourself, without having to call in outside help.

Let's go through these one at a time, and you'll see how simple it is to keep your engine happy.

Clean Fuel

Just like your car, engines burn fuel to run. Most inboard engines on sailboats, trawlers, and larger power vessels burn diesel fuel. Many smaller boats with inboard engines and virtually all outboard engines burn gasoline. This, then, is one of the most critical things you should know about your engine: does it take diesel or gas? Put the wrong type in your tank, and you could ruin your engine. If you go to a fuel pier and the attendant doesn't ask if you want diesel or gas, be sure to check which hose he gives you. Never assume it's the right one.

Engines are precision machines. While we can put all kinds of junk in our stomach and tolerate it to a point, engines will balk at the smallest bit of foreign matter in their systems. But it's not just dirt that will contaminate your fuel. Plain old water can ruin your engine's day.

How does water get into your fuel? You may get a bad batch of fuel at the pier, although this is less usual in the U.S., Canada, or Europe than in tropical and third world countries. If you put extra fuel in small jerry jugs that sit in the hot sun too long, they may collect enough condensation to affect the quality of your fuel. The other way to get water in your fuel is by human error. People intending to fill their water tanks have been known to put a water hose in the wrong deck fill. Oh yes, it can happen to anyone, and it's not a pretty scene. It's a good idea to ensure that helpful guests or crew know exactly which deck fill to use for each fluid.

There are several ways to prevent contamination of your fuel by either water or dirt:

- Make sure your deck fills are clearly labeled either "Fuel," "Water," or "Waste," and never, ever, get them confused.
- Make sure the fuel you buy is pure. The best way to do this is by going to a fuel dock that has a lot of traffic. The more fuel they

pump, the more often it gets changed. Fuel docks that serve working boats or sportsfishermen will usually have the best product.

• Make sure your tanks are clean. Older tanks can have a layer of sediment at the bottom. If you get into rough seas where your boat is rocking and rolling, you're likely to stir up all that gunk. Next thing you know, your fuel lines are clogged. This is what is known as "bad ju-ju." It's a good idea to have your fuel (and water) tanks cleaned every few years.

• On outboard engines, replace the fuel filter; on inboards, replace or clean your fuel filters/screens. The most common cause of a sudden engine stoppage is a clogged fuel filter. Most inboards have primary and secondary fuel filters. If you take a look at your engine and how the filters are placed, you'll see that they're located so that the fuel will go through the filter before it gets to the cylinders. This stops contaminants before they get to the most sensitive parts. In most Racor-type filters, you can see the dirty fuel, maybe with visible sediment, that collects in a clear reservoir at the bottom of the filter assembly. You'll also be able to see any water that may have collected. Since water doesn't mix with fuel and is heavier, it will settle at the bottom of the filter bowl. Some installations come with a vacuum gauge on top of the filter and/or an alarm to let you know when the filter starts to get clogged. At that point, replace the filter before the engine stops for lack of clean fuel.

Clean Oil

There are a lot of moving parts on an engine. Where there's movement between two objects, friction results. Without a lubricant, two things will happen to the rubbing objects: They'll heat up and they'll wear down, neither one of which is desirable. This makes oil one of your engine's best friends.

Your engine has an oil reservoir—a sump at the bottom of the engine. A pump will distribute the oil to all the needy parts and keep it humming. That same oil will flow through the whole system over and over, picking up bits of dirt and crud along the way. If you've ever compared engine oil straight from the container with the stuff that comes out during an oil change, it's hard to believe it's the same substance. New engine oil is generally honey-colored. Used oil is black and has a carbon smell.

Find out where your engine's dipstick is and pull it out. Run a paper towel over the end to clean it off, then put the stick back. Take it out again and this time look at the end of the stick. You want to check for two things: Is there enough oil in the system, as indicated by the lines on the dipstick, and how does the oil look?

If the level is too low, simply add more to the crankcase. Don't know how to do that? Ask someone to show you where the fill cap is. Remove the lid. Be sure to note if you had to unscrew it or just pull it loose. Add the type of oil recommended in your engine's user manual, being careful not to fill it too far, and replace the cap just as you removed it. If it is a screw-in cap, use only your hand to tighten it, not a wrench. Nothing to it.

If the oil on the end of the dipstick is clear, you're doing fine. If it's looking pretty black, you might want to think about having the oil changed (or learn how to do it yourself, if you're so inclined). In any case, a good rule of thumb is to change the oil after every 100 hours of engine use, so be sure to keep track of when it was last changed.

If you have an inboard engine, you likely have an engine oil pressure gauge. Know where it is and what a normal reading is for your engine, as indicated in the engine manual. Should your oil pressure alarm ever go off, immediately shut down your engine and find out what the problem is. Failure to do so could severely damage your engine.

Cooling Water

Burning fuel . . . friction . . . moving parts . . . all of these combine to produce heat. Without a method of cooling things down, your engine could overheat to the point of failure. All engines, whether inboard or outboard, diesel or gasoline, use water as the cooling agent.

Water in your fuel is bad, but engine cooling water never comes in contact with your fuel. Engines are designed very cleverly. Look closely and you'll see a variety of hoses of different sizes. Some carry fuel, and others carry water through all the hottest parts to absorb all that excess heat and cart it off.

If you have an outboard engine, the cooling water system pretty much takes care of itself. There's a small pump under the lid that sucks in seawater straight through a hole in the engine itself, and pushes it past the hot spots. The water that spits out of your outboard while it's running is the cooling water being discharged back to the source after it's done its job. Watch somebody working on an outboard that's not mounted on a boat, and you'll see that they've rigged a way to provide cooling water while testing the engine's operation.

Inboard engines also suck in cooling water from outside the hull, be it fresh water from a lake or salt water from the sea. This water, called raw water, comes in through a hose connected to a hole in the bottom of the boat. Through-hulls such as this have valves with a handle so that you can allow or shut off the flow of water. If the handle is in line with the hose, the valve is open. If it's perpendicular to the hose, it's closed.

As mentioned in the chapter on safety, you should make it a point to know where every through-hull is on your boat. Ensure that each hose has not just one, but two hose clamps on all of your through-hull hoses. Hose clamps should be stainless steel, tight, and rust-free. Raw water hoses are generally large, and you can imagine what would happen if yours came loose from the through-hull fitting while the valve was open. Hose clamps are good insurance against this, but so is closing the through-hull if you won't be using the engine for a while.

Because the inlet hose is so large, gunk in the water, such as seaweed, can get sucked inside. Your inboard engine system has a sea water strainer installed to catch debris before it goes too far. This strainer should be checked and cleaned regularly.

Inboards actually have two very distinct cooling water systems. A reservoir on the engine holds engine cooling water mixed with antifreeze/coolant. This flows via a completely closed system through water jackets around the engine. After the coolant water has absorbed the engine's heat, it passes through a heat exchanger, where it flows next to tubes filled with the raw water. The raw water absorbs the heat from the engine cooling water, then flows back to the sea.

The raw water discharge hose is equally as large as the inlet hose, but it discharges above the waterline. This is why water spits out the side or transom of your boat every time you run your inboard engine. This overboard discharge is the raw water, carrying off the engine heat, mixed with engine exhaust gases.

It only takes minutes for an engine to critically overheat without cooling water. Before starting your engine, always ensure that raw water is able to flow through the system. Friends of ours on a boat named *Starburst* learned this lesson the hard way. They hadn't been under way in some time and were going to join us and another boat for a weekend rendezvous at a favorite anchorage. We were running behind and were still messing about on *Liberty* after the other two boats left the marina.

We happened to have our VHF radio turned on and overheard one couple hail the other. It seemed that *Starburst*'s engine had died. They had their sails up, but there was hardly enough wind to fill them, so they were adrift. We listened in while the two boats discussed what might be wrong. It didn't take long to figure out.

Having been so long without getting under way, *Starburst*'s captain had forgotten to open the raw water inlet valve. Without that critical cooling water, the small rubber impeller on their raw water pump had dried up and broken. Engines don't like when this happens, and *Starburst*'s had shown its displeasure in a very noticeable way. With no wind and no cooling water, that boat wasn't going anywhere.

Water pump impellers, like fuel filters, are one of those items that should be near the top of your spare parts list. *Starburst* didn't have an extra one aboard. (This was strike two, after not checking the valve in the first place). Luckily, because we hadn't yet left the marina and were listening in on the conversation, we were able to pick one up for them before getting under way. We caught up to them shortly thereafter and passed the impeller across to them on a line. Within minutes of inserting the new impeller, *Starburst*'s engine came back to life and they were able to join the rest of us by sunset.

The three couples discussed *Starburst*'s troubles over dinner that evening. The unfortunate captain jabbered on, but his mate was silent. It was clear she knew little about engines and therefore had been unable to provide much help when things went sour. Unfortunately, if she'd known the basics about their cooling system, she might have saved the day simply by checking one crucial valve or looking over the side for raw water discharge before they left the pier. After all, there were two sets of eyes on that boat, not just one.

The following will ensure that your engine's cooling water system continues to operate well:

- Never start your engine without ensuring the through-hull is open.
- Once you've started the engine, check your overboard discharge to ensure water is coming out.
- Check your impeller from time to time (maybe once a year) to make sure none of the rubber blades have bent, cracked, or broken off.

- Clean the sea water strainer once a month, or more often if you're in an area with lots of weeds.
- Take the cap off your coolant reservoir from time to time and top it off as needed.
- Carry spare impellers.
- Ensure all hoses and clamps are tight and in good condition.
- Keep an eye on your cooling water temperature gauge, if you have one. Consult your engine's manual to find out what a normal temperature is for your model. If the cooling water alarm ever goes off, shut down your engine immediately.

Air

Car engines are air-cooled. They use fans and radiators to cool them. Boat engines don't use air for cooling, but like cars, they require air for combustion. Whether diesel or gasoline powered, engines need both fuel and air to keep the fuel burning inside the cylinders. Just like fuel and water, this air needs to be clean. Lucky for you, your engine comes with an air filter that will pretty much take care of itself. For once you get a break— you don't need to check it but every few years.

There's no reason for your engine to be a mystery. Sit down sometime with someone who knows how they work, be it your partner or somebody else, and have a "show and tell" session. Point to the various parts and ask, "What does this do?" and "What's that for?" Within minutes, what before seemed like a baffling jumble of hoses and metal will become the orderly arrangement of parts that work together to move your boat through the water.

Learn the location of the things you should check on a regular basis: fuel filters, oil fill cap, dipstick, coolant fill cap, cooling water hoses, pumps, impellers, and through-hull valves. Check the critical ones each time before you get under way. There's safety in numbers, so with more than just one person checking for problems, you're more likely to catch problems before they occur.

Don't rely on your partner to remember everything involved in the care and feeding of your engine. When you learn what makes it tick and purr, you can participate in ensuring that yours remains "the little engine that could," instead of becoming the weight at the end of a mooring line.

18

SYSTEMS

The larger the boat, the more complex it is. Rowboats and sailing dinghies have little more than the hull and oars or a sail to worry about. Move up a size or two, and before you know it, your boat is as complicated as a house.

The systems aboard a bigger boat are, in fact, quite similar to those in a house. Both have electricity and plumbing that provide comfort and convenience. The difference lies in the maintenance requirements and layout. Houses are dry and they don't move around. Boats shake, rattle, roll, and get wet, inside and out. Houses have lots of room for hoses, wires, and machinery. On a boat, you squeeze and bend things into every available space.

The result is a maze of wires and hoses that can be pretty intimidating if you don't know what you're looking at. A bit of close scrutiny, however, will reveal that the wiring and plumbing on a boat are actually quite simple. It doesn't take a mechanical genius to understand how the systems on your boat work. But why would you want to?

Self sufficiency, self-edification, and saving money are a few reasons that come to mind.

Our boat has a reverse-cycle air conditioner that we use if we're in a marina and it's too hot to sleep. It usually works fine, but one day it shut itself off within five minutes of our turning it on. I flipped the circuit breaker on the electrical panel and got the same result.

Now, if Ty and I hadn't known anything about the air conditioner and its installation, we might have been tempted to call in outside help. In fact, we mentioned to the fellow in the slip across the dock from ours that our unit was on the fritz, and he perked right up. It seems his air conditioner had been broken for weeks.

"I'll bet it's the compressor," he said. "Why don't we get a mechanic out here and we can share the cost?"

The thought of needing a new compressor had also occurred to us, but we declined our friend's offer until we could troubleshoot the problem ourselves. Troubleshooting is a detective-like process of elimination. It requires a step-by-step progression from the simplest solution to the most difficult.

The first thing we checked was the power source. Was the shore power cord loose at the pier? No. Ok, what about our electrical panel? Was the main shore power breaker in the "on" position, as well as the air conditioner switch itself? Yes, but turning it on caused the ammeter to steadily rise past its normal ten amps, peg out at fifty, and trip the breaker.

So now we'd eliminated simple electrical problems as the cause of the malfunction. It was time to look at the plumbing. Just like engines, air conditioners on boats get hot and use cooling water to carry off the heat. Perhaps our unit was overheating.

I went out on deck and peered over the side while Ty flipped the air conditioner switch. I watched for water to exit the overboard discharge through-hull.

Nothing.

The ammeter went through its now-familiar pegging routine, and not a drop of cooling water came out. Now we were getting closer to solving the mystery.

Up came the floorboards for access to the maze of hoses and valves. First stop: the salt-water strainer. Ty closed the through-hull, noting a little resistance, then opened the strainer assembly. He removed the wire mesh basket and cleaned out a little gunk and a few barnacle particles, then put the strainer basket back in place, leaving the top of the strainer open. We watched as I opened the through-hull valve. Since the strainer was below the waterline, seawater should have flowed up through the open top of the strainer assembly, but there was no water flow. It didn't take Sherlock Holmes to figure out there was blockage somewhere leading up to the strainer.

Moving from simplest to most difficult, Ty went topside. We thought that perhaps a plastic bag or other piece of garbage had gotten sucked against the hull, blocking the raw water inlet. Using our boat hook, he swept under the hull. Inside, I rotated the though-hull valve several times, leaving it in the open position again. Still no flow. Now it was time for tools.

Ty used a straight screwdriver to loosen the hose clamps, then pulled off the hose between the though-hull valve and the strainer. A red liquid trickled out. We looked at each other, puzzled. The liquid looked like hydraulic fluid, but that made no sense at all. There was no reason for there to be anything but clear water in the hose, and especially no reason for something red. Shrugging that mystery aside, Ty peered through the two-foot length of hose he'd just removed. It was clear. We had now narrowed down the location of the cooling water blockage to the through-hull itself.

It's always a little disconcerting looking at a valve that is the only thing standing between you and water up to your armpits, but with the handle back in the closed position, Ty carefully unscrewed the elbow connector on top. I shined the flashlight onto his work area, and the two of us leaned in for a closer look. He pulled off the connector, revealing the cause of the blockage.

The shock of the unexpected and a stomach-turning stench sent both of us tumbling backward in a scene straight out of Laurel and Hardy. We gaped with revulsion into the single beady eye of a dead eel that had managed to swim a full four inches past the through-hull before becoming irrevocably stuck. The puzzle of the lack of cooling water was solved, as was the mysterious red liquid and the resistance Ty had felt when he initially closed and re-opened the valve—it was eel blood.

Yuck.

Our slimy intruder had done as good a job as the emergency wood plug lying in the bilge next to the through-hull.

Using a paper towel, Ty pulled out the offending eel-plug. Unfortunately, what remained of the carcass continued to block the through-hull. What can't come in, must go out, so I shoved a second paper towel down and out through the hole in the hull with a long screwdriver. We now had water—lots of it—gushing through the inlet. A quick turn of the valve and all was well.

It was a simple matter to replace the connector and reattach the hose. When I flipped the switch for the air conditioner, it came on and stayed on. A check of the overboard discharge revealed a normal, steady flow of cooling water. We high-fived and congratulated ourselves on successfully solving the problem at no expense and with no outside help.

Mechanics aren't cheap. We would have paid big bucks for an air-conditioning technician to come out and tell us our problem wasn't the compressor, but an eel in our through-hull. It's surprising how many problems you can take care of, and even prevent, when you have a basic understanding of your boat's mechanical, electrical, and plumbing systems.

Electrical System Basics

My brother-in-law is an electrician. I have great respect for him and anyone who works with live wires for a living. As for me, I've learned the basics. I can change a light bulb and even wire in a new 12V lamp. The most important thing I know about electricity and boats is to be very, very careful when working with power cords, outlets, and live equipment.

In a house, you plug in your appliances and forget about them. Unless there's a thunderstorm or a truck hits a nearby telephone pole, your power source is constant and unchanging. Not so on a boat. Boats use two different types of electricity: alternating current (AC), the kind that comes from shore power, and direct current (DC), from batteries when under way.

Direct current aboard most boats is the 12-volt variety (some boats use 24-volt batteries). That's enough to start your engine and power things like lights and navigational instruments. If you get shocked by 12 volts, you'll feel a tingle for sure, but it won't kill you.

AC is different. Those thick yellow cords you use on your boat have 110 volts of electricity coursing through them as soon as they're attached to a live power source ashore. Hence, **Electrical Safety Lesson Number One**:

Always plug your shore power cord into the boat first, and the power source last. If you don't, you'll be carrying a live wire across the deck of an object that's floating in water. For obvious reasons, you don't want to do that.

As soon as you've connected your boat to the shore power outlet and energized the breaker on the pier, run below and look at your electrical panel. If a red light with the label "Reverse Polarity" is glowing, disconnect the shore power immediately. This means there's a problem in the wiring at your marina, which could severely damage your electrical equipment. Either change slips or call an electrician from the marina, but don't use the outlet until the problem is fixed.

When it comes time to disconnect from shore power, reverse the process. Always turn off the circuit breaker on the boat first, then the circuit breaker on the pier. Never disconnect a live cord from the boat first. Disconnect it from the outlet on the pier and then from your boat.

Electrical Safety Lesson Number Two

Always ensure all power sources are disconnected or turned off before working on any electrical equipment aboard your boat. I don't recommend you work on anything having 110V power at all. Period. Leave that to the experts. If for some reason you have to get at something on the back of your DC (battery) panel, don't take any chances. Even though, theoretically, the 12V system should be completely separate from the 110V, it often shares the same panel with 110 volts on the other side. It's best to disconnect shore power completely before doing any work on your 12-volt panel.

These safeguards are good to know even if you never pick up a pair of wire cutters or a voltage meter. If someone else is doing the work, you can at least be a safety observer. Keep these pointers in mind, and lessen the chance that somebody might get shocked.

While the back side of your electrical panel may remain a mystery, the front side should be as familiar to you as the dashboard on your car. In a house, if you blow a fuse, it's a simple matter of running to the fuse box and resetting the breaker that tripped from "off" to "on." Electrical panels on boats, being black and having lots of switches, may look intimidating, but they're no more complicated than your fuse box at home.

If you don't know what every switch, button, and dial on your boat's electrical panel is for, take five minutes to find out. Five minutes: that's all it takes to remove the mystery.

Most panels are divided into different sections for AC and DC power. Know how the circuit breakers should be configured for each panel. There is often a meter to show how many volts are flowing to the panel and another to indicate how much current the equipment you're using is drawing. The rows of switches are nothing more than on/off toggles. They work just like light switches at home.

The switches on a boat's 12V panel power a few nice-to-have amenities like cabin lights and perhaps a stereo or TV, but for the most part, the batteries power the equipment that's vital to your boat's operation: running and steaming lights, the anchor light, VHF, navigation instruments, water pumps, and bilge pumps. Bilge pumps should be in the "on" position all the time. You should be so familiar with all the switches that you can find them in a hurry and/or in the dark.

The 110V side of your panel will have switches to power any electrical outlets on your boat, plus the equipment onboard that uses 110 volts. This can include such things as the battery charger, hot water heater, refrigeration (if your system is 110 volts), inverter, and air conditioners. Some boats also have 110-volt stoves, washer-dryers, and watermakers.

110V is often referred to as "shore power," but a boat doesn't necessarily have to be pierside to run appliances requiring 110 volts. Generators, powered by either gasoline or diesel fuel, create AC electricity aboard larger vessels. They come in various sizes, can be portable or permanently installed, and produce varying amounts of output. Even smaller boats can convert DC electricity from 12V batteries into 110V AC electricity through the use of an inverter. These range from small, portable units that plug into a cigarette lighter with enough power to run a laptop computer, to permanently installed inverters that can run one or more household appliances at once.

An inverter will draw down the batteries quickly because 110V appliances are very power-hungry. Typical high-load appliances include microwaves and hair dryers, which, thankfully, only run for a short period of time. Nevertheless, be aware of how much power you're using and keep your batteries charged up.

Dead batteries are never good. It's one thing not to be able to read in the dark. It's another not to be able to start your engine. After a night at anchor, you can't exactly ask for a jump start from the guy in the next parking space. If you have only one battery on board, the solution is to take it ashore in a dinghy or in someone else's boat and recharge it. Or you can find a brand new one at a store, pull out your credit card and say, "Charge it." The end result will be the same.

Most boats with more than one battery have a battery selector switch. This is usually a big, round, red thing with a black knob that has three positions: 1, 2, or "All." One of the two numbers is the engine starting battery. The other number will be the "house battery," for all those other things that normally run off DC power. Know which switch is which on your boat.

The "All" switch connects to both the engine starting battery and the house battery at the same time. Should your engine starting battery die, you can turn the switch to the "All" position and crank her up. Be aware, however, that when you do this, you're drawing down all your batteries at once. Luckily, as long as your engine alternator is working, it should charge both battery banks, so your engine starting battery should be recharged and usable in a couple of hours.

The Poop on Plumbing

While electricians have my respect for working with high voltage, I admire plumbers for a totally different reason. They deal with all those nasty things that most people won't go near with a ten-foot boat hook.

While some plumbing jobs aboard a boat are messy, many deal with nothing more than water hoses, valves, and clamps. The amount of effort you decide to contribute to your boat's plumbing system is up to you, but when it's your boat, too, it pays to at least know how things work.

Ty went out of town one week and I had a lot of time on my hands. Our electric toilet had been acting up, and having had several recent successes in the boat maintenance department, I decided to do something about it. That evening Ty called me from his hotel.

"Did you have a good day?" he asked.

"Pretty good," I replied casually. "I went for a run, had lunch, then I replaced the electric motor on the head." (This was another one of those boat jobs where electric and plumbing systems interact).

There was a long pause, followed by the two words which I knew would follow.

"You what???"

I have to say, that felt pretty good.

While I hadn't exactly enjoyed handling those stinky hoses and spending hours on my knees before the throne, I loved knowing that I was doing something I never thought I could. The further into the job I got, the more I realized how simple it was.

I'm well aware that working on a marine head is something most women neither aspire nor desire to do. Most men probably don't relish working with plugged drains and smelly hoses, either, but there's a reason guys enjoy messing about with tools: they get instant gratification and tremendous satisfaction from taking something that doesn't work and fixing it.

Fixing that head was certainly gratifying. When I tightened up the final hose clamp, put my foot on the pedal, and the toilet actually flushed, I got all choked up. Ok, laugh if you must, but plumbing is a typical blue job, and I'd successfully turned it purple (You know, pink plus blue equals purple . . . .)

You may never fix a clogged hose or replace a pump, but there are a few plumbing basics that all boat owners should be familiar with:

• Know where your through-hulls are and inspect them regularly. I've brought this up several times because it's such a critical safety issue. Ensure all hoses leading to holes in your boat are double hose-clamped and have a wooden plug nearby in case of flooding. Rotate the handles at least monthly to keep the valves from freezing in one position. Close all through-hulls if you're going to leave the boat for any length of time.

• Know where your bilge pumps are and ensure they're working. Check your bilges on a regular basis and at least every other hour while under way. There's usually a small amount of water in any bilge, but if you notice that the level has risen, immediately track down the source. Keep bilge pump switches in the "on" position at all times.

• Be sure that bilge pump and shower sump discharge hoses are installed with a vented loop. Hoses that are meant to dump water overboard can siphon, or unintentionally allow water to flow back into the boat. To prevent this, the hose should be run a couple of feet above the water line, then looped back down to its above-water through-hull. Having a vent at the highest point in the loop prevents siphoning.

• Clean your sea water strainers regularly, particularly if you live in an area with lots of sea grass or weeds. Our generator has shut down twice because it overheated when the strainer became clogged with eel grass or weeds, even though we clean the strainers once a month. The areas we were cruising just happened to have particularly bad weed problems. You'll find strainers in the sea water lines leading to engines, generators, watermakers, and refrigeration and air conditioning systems. There will also be some in your fresh (drinking) water lines. Know where yours are.

- Ensure that nothing goes in the head except toilet paper and matter that has already passed through a human body. This is common knowledge among most boaters, but don't assume your guests know it. Marine heads have smaller discharge hoses than the pipes on your toilet at home, and pumps that are easily clogged. Put anything in them that's not supposed to go there and you're asking for trouble.

It's not just the introduction of foreign objects that will clog your head. Over time, the interior walls of the discharge hose will get a buildup of scale—a mixture of salt deposits and human waste. Just like the accumulation of plaque on human arteries, this blockage gradually decreases the interior diameter of the hose until you have a total blockage. Finding yourself on a boat without an operational head is similar to atherosclerosis—both can cause cardiac arrest.

Head hoses should be cleaned before they get to this point. It's really quite simple to do. First, close the overboard discharge valve. Unscrew the hose clamps and detach the hoses. If they're hard to get off, aim a hair dryer or heat gun at the point where they're sticking for about thirty seconds and try again. Once removed, carefully carry the hoses outside and beat them against the side of the dock to break up the scale. After the majority of the gunk has broken loose, flush the hoses with fresh water. Put them back in place and tighten down the hose clamps.

Mission accomplished.

The frequency with which a boat owner has to perform this smelly, messy job depends on the amount of use your head gets. Liveaboards may need to clean out the hoses once a year, whereas weekenders could get by with once every several years.

No matter how long you go between cleanings, ladies, if you get to the point where you're the one clearing clogged head hoses, I applaud you—you have truly accepted the concept of equality afloat. If, however, your gallant partner offers to do the job, this is one time when you're lucky that chivalry isn't dead.

In either case, you now at least know how to do the job. You also have the knowledge to ensure that other parts of your plumbing system are installed correctly and used safely. Combine this with your new understanding of how your boat's electrical system works, and you'll never again be in the dark.

Congratulations. You have what it takes to be a full partner in your boat's operation.

PART III

Under Way

19

Working as a Team

Have you ever gone on a trip alone or experienced something new and exciting by yourself? If so, you may have felt that something was missing. Solitude is nice for a while, but I've always found that things are far more fun when they're shared.

Boating is no different. A solo passage can be blissfully peaceful, but go away for too long and you might find yourself wishing for a little companionship. How much more pleasant things are when you can look over at a person whose company you enjoy and say, "It just doesn't get any better than this."

Not only is it nice to share your time on the water, but things are also far easier with four hands than with two. You know: one person docks the boat, while the other handles the lines. One tends to the anchor, while the other mans the helm. One pours the wine, while the other gets out the cheese and crackers.

The downside to companionship afloat is that we don't all do things the same way, nor can we read each other's minds. While we may think our partner should know what we want or how we intend to do things, it just doesn't work that way. This can lead to problems on a boat, where so many things require instant action and cooperation.

Members of sports teams know how important it is to work together. Everyone has a role and each values the others' contributions. They practice their moves until every action flows smoothly, like a well-oiled machine. They know what to expect from each other and share a common goal.

When you go boating with your partner, you are a team. You share the same goals: to have fun and be safe. You can't achieve either, however, if you're working at cross purposes, if you don't know what the other is doing, or worse yet, if you're yelling at each other.

To be a contributing member of the team, you first have to know what you're doing. Having read the book to this point, you have a good foundation. Now you need to continue your education, and apply and practice what you've learned.

Unfortunately, no matter how much you know, or how good your skills are, if you're on a different wavelength than your partner, things can go awry. The other half of the teamwork equation, therefore, is good communication. Bear in mind that if your partner is male, he may not speak the same language as you do to begin with. This is all the more reason to work on your communication skills afloat.

You and your partner should agree upon how best to do specific boating tasks and should each try to perform them the same way. This cuts down frustration and simplifies effort. If you want your double braid line coiled in figure eights, you should both coil them that way. If your partner hangs the fenders from the rail with a simple clove hitch, you should follow suit. While it's good to be flexible for those times when "the way we've always done it" won't work, maintaining consistency ensures that things will be done more quickly and more safely.

During certain boating activities, however, your actions will vary depending on external forces. On all boats, the most common examples include entering or leaving a slip or pier, anchoring, and picking up a mooring. On sailboats, you can add raising and lowering sails, reefing, and jibing. In all of these cases, the steps you take will differ slightly each time depending on the wind and current, your location, and the depth of the water.

The best team response to an ever-changing environment is to discuss everything before you do it, with good communication as your goal. That's my Navy training talking, but military folks know the value of good planning. The best way to make sure you both know who's going to do what and in what order you're going to do it, is to talk it over in advance.

Say you're going back to your marina at the end of a nice day on the water. You've been doing this all season, but just the same, while you're still in open water you conduct a purposeful discussion about what's going to happen at the dock. As you rig the fenders, you ask and answer the following questions:

- Who's going to drive and who's going to handle lines?
- How are the wind and current going to affect our landing and how should we compensate?
- Which line should we get over first?
- Is there anything else we need to think of?
- Ready? Set?

Go!

Getting ready to pick up a mooring or reef the sails? It doesn't matter how many times you've done this drill. Before one of you steps out of the cockpit, discuss exactly what steps each of you is going to take. When you're ready to go and you actually execute what you've just discussed, both of you know exactly what each of you is doing. There's no confusion, no quibbling, and no surprises.

Using checklists for common tasks is a great way to ensure nobody forgets a critical task. When you get distracted or are in a hurry, it's amazing how easy it is to overlook something you've done a hundred times before. If our friends on *Starburst* had used a predeparture checklist, they wouldn't have forgotten to open their raw water inlet valve. A quick review before getting under way would have saved them from burning up their impeller and falling several hours behind.

Appendix A is a predeparture checklist. Appendix B is a checklist for securing your boat after being under way. I recommend you and your partner use these as a guide and tailor them to your specific boat. Keep them in a handy place on your boat where you won't forget them. Come up with other checklists as needed and confirm with each other that together you've completed each step for whatever task you're undertaking. Never assume anything.

Even when you think you're communicating well, it's possible to be misinterpreted. Ty and I learned this valuable lesson while sailing into Boston Harbor. The entrance channel was crowded. Our guide book cautioned small boats to stay clear of big commercial traffic—a warning I found quite unnecessary. An enormous supertanker chugged past us, heading to sea, and I instinctively pulled to the far right side of the channel.

While Ty studied the electronic chart at the navigation table below, I verified our position on the paper chart by my side. We were approaching the southern tip of Deer Island. A light there marked a shoal I'd be wise to avoid. On my chart, the navigation aid stood out from others nearby. Squiggly gray lines in a circle around the red symbol indicated rocks at the base of the light. Sure enough, I could make out a towering light just off the starboard bow.

Ty popped his head up through the companionway. "Don't come too close to that light up ahead."

"Roger that," I replied. "I see it."

I knew why he was warning me. If I cut the corner too closely, the fathometer would go from fifty feet to four in a mere boat length.

The navigable channel was half a mile wide just opposite the light. Normally, I would have come left and run directly down the center, but a tug towing a large barge was headed for the same spot I was, just off my port beam. Technically, I had the right of way, but I could maneuver a lot easier than the tug could. Looking at the chart, I figured I was on a good course to comfortably clear the shoal and still give the tug plenty of room.

Just as I rounded the light, Ty popped his head up again. He looked over the starboard side, blinked, and did a double-take. He shouted an expletive, then ducked back below.

I looked at the fathometer. As far as I could see, everything was under control. But something told me I might want to come hard left. Now.

I maneuvered more toward the center of the channel. I was closer to the tug than I would have liked, but the water was definitely deeper here.

"What's your depth?" Ty asked, scrambling back into the cockpit.

"Fifty-three feet."

Ty looked at the rocky light, then did a 360-degree scan of the horizon. When his eyes came back to rest on mine, they were stony.

"Suzanne," he said ominously, from a mere two feet away, "what part of 'don't-come-too-close-to-the-light' didn't you understand?"

In spite of the cool fall air, I grew instantly hot as a mixture of fear, anger, embarrassment, and shame duked it out in my head. What had gone wrong? Nothing, as far as I could see. I'd done exactly as he'd said. I didn't think I'd come too close to the light, but Ty sure thought I did. He thought I'd endangered the boat.

Then, suddenly, I realized what the problem was. It was a classic example of he-thought-she-thought. When you ask or tell someone to do something, the person on the receiving end doesn't necessarily interpret it the same way you intend it to come across. It all depends on how it's worded.

Ty had told me not to come too close to the light. But what exactly did that mean? It was now clear that "too close" meant something very different to him than it did to me. When I asked him exactly how far away from the light he intended for me to stay, he said, "One hundred yards."

Well, my goodness . . . In my mind, "not too close" was about 100 feet.

Luckily, we didn't learn that lesson the hard way and end up on the rocks. As we sailed on into the harbor, I realized I'd been as guilty as he had of not quantifying things when communicating. How many times had I said, "You need to come right just a little"?

If you tell your partner to "come right just a little," how far will he turn the wheel? You may want him to come right five degrees, but "just a little" may mean fifteen degrees to him. In a narrow channel, ten degrees can make a big difference. If you're the one giving an instruction, be as specific as possible. If you're the one on the receiving end, and there's room for interpretation, ask for clarification: "Just what exactly do you mean by 'look at that big ship heading for us?'"

If something doesn't seem right to you, it probably isn't. Learn to trust your instincts. Even if you're not as experienced as your partner, your intuition will often alert you to dangers. Never hesitate to question things if you have any doubts that you're about to do something unsafe.

A good habit to get into while working together is for both you and your partner to repeat whatever the other says when giving directions. For example, if you're navigating and you tell your partner at the helm to come right twenty degrees, he should say, "Coming right twenty degrees." If you're sailing and he says, "Slack the mainsheet," you should immediately reply, "Slacking the mainsheet" as you do so. This type of back-and-forth communication not only acknowledges that you heard each other, but it ensures that you heard each other correctly.

Clear communication is important, but there may be times when the message is all too clear. Partners yelling and cursing at their mates can be a huge detractor from the main reason you go out on a boat—to have a good time.

An important point to keep in mind is that raised voices are not always angry voices. It's hard to hear over engines, howling wind, and flapping sails. It took me a while to learn this. Quite often when we hoisted our sails, Ty would stand at the mast and shout back to me at the helm things like, "Come right!" or "Slack the mainsheet!" I interpreted his tone as one of anger, when it was nothing more than his attempt to be heard above the luffing main.

"Don't yell at me!" I'd shout back, with real anger. Naturally, he'd shout back, "I'm not yelling at you!"

We only had to repeat this scene about fifty times before I finally got it.

Yelling can also be a response to stress. Certain situations on a boat, such as docking, are inherently more stressful than others:

An acquaintance of mine, the president of a major sailboat manufacturing company, was standing next to an empty slip one day when a couple who had bought one of his boats approached the pier. The man was at the helm and the woman stood at the bow, dock line in hand. The slip was wide, and the woman repeatedly threw the line and missed. Three times the man backed out and tried again, and each time his voice got louder and his language more coarse. On the third try, he yelled at his wife, "Get the damn line around the piling already!"

"I'm trying," she answered, her voice quavering.

Seeing the woman was close to tears, Ted glared at the man and said, "If you'd drive the damn boat better, she could get the damn line around the damn piling."

His comment had the desired effect. The man's red face showed he got the message.

As we discussed, talking over how you're going to handle docking, anchoring, and other stressful situations before you do them can eliminate a lot of the potential for stress-based anger. But some people will yell no matter what. If all else fails, tell your partner how much his yelling detracts from your enjoyment of your boat. If he still yells at you, maybe it's time to either get your own boat or find a new mate.

Aim to be on equal footing with your partner. Know what the other is doing and why. Work in harmony so that you can anticipate your mate's moves. Recognize the importance of clear communication and leave nothing open to interpretation.

When you and your partner work well as a team, boating becomes the pleasant activity it's meant to be.

20

Where You Go From Here

Have you ever noticed how certain people on the VHF will address whomever they're talking to as "Captain?" No matter if they hear a man's voice or a woman's, bridge tenders will say, "Bring her on up, Cap," or marina staff will ask, "How many nights will you be staying, Captain?"

If that's happened to you, it feels pretty good, doesn't it? There's something about that word "captain" that brings to mind knowledge, experience, authority, and a jaunty little hat with gold braid on it. Ok, skip the cheesy hat, but there's no reason you can't claim the title as well as any man. To earn money as a captain, you need a license issued by the Coast Guard. To be the captain of your own vessel, you simply need to assume the role and accept the responsibility.

Unless you've been reading this book by flashlight in a closet, or hiding it in your underwear drawer, your partner may have picked up on the fact that you're interested in getting more involved in boating. Discuss the new things you've learned with him. Talk about how you can take on a bigger role aboard your boat. Even if you're not yet ready to be co-captain and simply want to try some new duties, impress upon him the importance of your getting hands-on experience.

There may be certain tasks aboard your boat that your partner currently handles that don't interest you at all. Strive to at least know how to do them if you had to. When you see your mate plotting a course or studying a weather chart, ask yourself, "Could I do that if he weren't here?" If the answer is no, take the initiative and find out how. Either get him to show you, study it on your own, or ask someone else, but don't be content to remain uninformed.

Sign up for lessons to improve those skills which need improvement. Join a boating group to keep your enthusiasm charged. There are a number of organizations dedicated strictly to women boaters. Some are on the national level, but there may be a regional group in your own area. Search for them online or see Appendix D for a sample of the types of groups out there.

The things you've learned here about boating are the tip of the iceberg. There's a lot more under the surface than what we've covered. I've introduced you to eleven distinct facets of seamanship. Some of the topics go deeper than others, but now that you know what's under the surface, I hope you'll take a deep breath, dive down, and have a closer look.

Choose one subject or many, but continue to learn and improve your skills. Appendix C includes some of my favorite books to help you in your journey. Appendix D is a list of websites you may find useful.

The more competent you become on the water, the more fun you'll have. But be warned—if you really get into this boating thing, you may come down with BBS: the Bigger Boat Syndrome. No matter how happy you may be with your current boat, there's always another one out there that looks as if it might just be a little more fun to own.

While it's exciting shopping for boats, be careful not to fall for a boat just because it has a great interior. That's exactly what boat designers expect women to do.

Don't head straight for the salon when you step aboard. Take a good look at the deck first (if for no other reason than to shock the broker). How easy will it be to move around in any kind of sea? Does it flex when you jump on it? Are the fittings and hardware in good condition or are they rusted and cracked?

How is the boat built? Is the hull bulletproof, or kind of thin? Depending on how you're going to use the boat, you may be able to get by with a lighter vessel. Inshore and coastal boats don't need to be as sturdy as those bound for sea.

When shopping for our cruising boat, we went aboard one sailboat with an interior that was nicer than my house. I was in lust with that boat. I was all ready to plunk down a deposit when a very knowledgeable friend's comment stopped me in my tracks. "If you hit something with that boat, it'll sink within two minutes." Yikes. Scratch that one.

What kind of upkeep will the boat you're considering need? Is there a lot of wood topside that looks great now, but will need to be varnished within half a year? If you don't mind varnishing, maybe topside teak accents are for you. If you'd rather spend your time on your boat under way than sanding and scraping, set your sights on a different vessel.

Once inside, look closely at storage capacity. Poke around and ask yourself where you'd put things like clothes, food, and tools. How much fuel and water will the boat carry? If you only plan to go on day hops or short weekend trips, you won't need much. If your goal is long-term cruising, you'll want all you can get.

Beyond the pretty cushions and the nice layout, how does the engine look? Is it going to get you where you're going, or cost you an arm and a leg down the river to repair or replace?

Go shopping armed with a list of things you want and don't want in a boat. Use your current boat or those you've previously been aboard for comparison. The perfect boat for you may not exist, but a list will help keep you focused when emotion overcomes reason.

If you've never owned your own boat or are going for a totally different type than the one you now have, try chartering the kind you're interested in. Not only will you have a great vacation, but you'll also learn how a different boat handles and if it suits your needs.

Whether you're in the market for a new boat or are perfectly content with the one you own, you now know enough about boating to be dangerous. I don't mean that you're not safe to go out on the water. Quite the opposite. With the things you've learned here, there's nothing to stop you and nobody holding you back but yourself. There's no reason why your partner should enjoy boating any more than you do.

No longer do you have to settle for merely going along for the ride. You have what it takes to be a fully contributing member of your crew, if not the captain. Take the helm with confidence and experience the pride of doing so.

Pushing yourself beyond your comfort zone isn't easy. It's far more comfortable to continue living with things the way you've always done them. But what's the fun in that? Where's the challenge?

Be bold!

Only by taking risks do we grow.

Postscript

While reading the latest bulletin from the Seven Seas Cruising Association, I came across a story about the owner of a pleasure boat who experienced a medical emergency on board. His treatment was delayed because his partner was unable to maneuver the vessel alongside a nearby pier.

The author of the article confirmed what I've expressed repeatedly in this book. Accidents and injuries can happen anywhere. It's vital that you be able to handle your boat and all safety equipment by yourself. This is not something you can simply think about doing—it takes hands-on practice.

Ironically, the very day after I completed the first draft of this book, my husband pulled his back while aboard our boat. He could barely move for three days. When the wind shifted and our anchorage became too rolly for comfort, it was time to practice what I'd been preaching for the past two-hundred-plus pages. It was up to me to single-hand our boat to a more comfortable location.

Moving the boat required raising the anchor, maneuvering under power and sail, navigating, applying the Rules of the Road to avoid other vessels, choosing a good anchorage, and setting the hook. Thankfully, I was able to do all of this with no problems and with a big smile on my face at the end of the day.

I hope that (minus the medical issues) you, too, will soon be able to say the same.

I've stressed throughout these pages that getting more involved in your boat will increase your enjoyment. There's no doubt that's true. But fun is only one of the reasons for taking on a bigger role. Safety is critical.

Happily, whether you learn and do more for personal pleasure or for the safety of everyone aboard, the pride and self-satisfaction you'll experience will be the same.

APPENDIX A

PRE-DEPARTURE CHECKLIST

- Check your waterline and bilges to ensure the boat is not taking on water.
- Turn on VHF.
- Double check weather on VHF and visually.
- Check tide/current tables.
- Turn on instruments.
- Check fuel level.
- Check engine oil.
- Turn off shore power at the electrical panel.
- Take in power cords.
- Stow all items securely for sea.
- Put chart, binoculars, and GPS in cockpit.
- Ensure engine through-hull is open.
- Warm up engine/check for leaks and cooling water discharge, ensure all gauge readings are within limits.
- Gently test forward and reverse.
- Take in all lines except bow and stern lines.
- Set remaining bow and stern lines with a single open loop around cleats.
- Check current and wind and talk through departure one last time.
- Get under way by slipping loops off cleats.

Appendix B

Securing the Boat Checklist

- Shut down engine.
- Secure and double up all dock lines, centering boat in slip.
- Turn off VHF radio and instruments.
- Close engine through-hull and others as desired.
- Connect power cords.
- Power up electrical panel.
- Ensure bilge pumps are turned on.
- Put chart, binoculars, and GPS below.
- Wash down deck.
- Close all hatches and ports.
- Lock boat.

APPENDIX C

RECOMMENDED READING

Boatowner's Mechanical and Electrical Manual, by Nigel Calder. (International Marine/McGraw-Hill, Camden, Maine, 3rd Edition, 2004.)

Many consider this the boat owner's "bible" when it comes to maintenance and repair. If you can't find how to do something in this book, it's probably time to call a mechanic. Includes excellent illustrations and troubleshooting guides.

The Care and Feeding of Sailing Crew, Cost Conscious Cruiser, Self-Sufficient Sailor, and any of the other books by cruisers Lin and Larry Pardey. (Distributed by Paradise Cay Publications, www.paracay.com)

The Pardeys share over forty years of lessons-learned in their many excellent books and videos about cruising. This intrepid couple epitomizes equality on board a boat.

Changing Course – A Woman's Guide to Choosing the Cruising Life, by Debra Ann Cantrell. (International Marine/McGraw-Hill, Camden, Maine, 2004.)

In trying to limit the number of books aboard my boat, I initially put this one in storage because I'd already read it. Six months into the cruising life I longed to re-read the sage advice Cantrell provides. Since my copy was buried in a box, I invested in a second copy. It was well worth it. Includes the results of a survey of over 100 cruising women and the common issues they face.

Chapman Piloting: Seamanship & Small Boat Handling, by Elbert S. Maloney. (Hearst Marine Books, New York, New York, updated every couple of years.)

I recommend this as the "text book" for my sailing students. It's a big book, but every page is packed with good information. A very comprehensive book on all aspects of seamanship for both powerboats and sailboats.

COLREGS Study Guide and Ready Reference, by Greg Szczurek. (Houston Marine Consultants, Inc. Second Edition, Houston, Texas, 1993.)

This small, spiral-bound version of the Rules of the Road is great to carry around and study whenever you have a few minutes. The full transcript of the Rules is at the back, but the main body of the book summarizes them nicely. Cleverly shows pictures of various lights at night, in a flashcard format, followed by a photo of what kind of vessel might actually be under those lights.

The Complete Book of Anchoring and Mooring, by Earl Hinz. (Cornell Maritime Press, Centreville, Maryland, 2001.)

While not the most riveting reading, if you want to know everything there is about anchoring, this is the book.

The Cruising Woman's Advisor: How to Prepare for the Voyaging Life, by Diana Jessie. (International Marine/McGraw-Hill, Camden, Maine, 1997.)

A great book for any woman thinking about going cruising. Covers all the major concerns and includes interviews with women cruisers.

Know Your Boat, by David Kroenke. (International Marine/McGraw-Hill, Camden, Maine, 2002.)

Kroenke really knows how to put boat systems into plain English. Written with great humor and cartoon-like illustrations, this book makes it fun to learn the mechanical and electrical aspects of your boat.

Living a Dream, by Suzanne Giesemann (Aventine Press, Chula Vista, California, 2005.)

In this memoir and cruising chronicle, I tell what it was like to be the aide to the chairman of the Joint Chiefs of Staff at the Pentagon on 9/11, and how that tragic day propelled me to go cruising sooner rather than later. The book gives an honest look at the humor and drama of first-year adjustments to the cruising life, and details our voyage to Nova Scotia and Newfoundland.

Men Are From Mars, Women Are From Venus, by John Gray. (Harper Collins, New York, 1992.)

This book may not have anything to do with the water, but if you're going to go boating with a man, it's definitely worth a read. When we moved aboard our boat, I had to get rid of most of my books. Not this one. I wouldn't be without this insightful relationship-saver.

Navigation Rules International-Inland (U.S. Department of Homeland Security/United States Coast Guard COMDTINST M16672.2C)

This is the actual Coast Guard-issued text of the Collision Regulations/Rules of the Road. Plenty of publishers have produced varying versions of the rules, but here you can read them straight from the source. Uses easy-to-understand language and includes good illustrations, unusual for a government publication.

Reed's Nautical Almanac, edited by Carl Herzog. (Thomas Reed Publications, Boston, Massachusetts, updated annually.)

Published annually with different editions for the different geographic regions of the U.S., Reed's is the "one-stop" source of navigation information for the entire coast, including tide and current tables and piloting data for the most common boating areas.

Reed's Nautical Companion: the Handbook to Complement Reed's Almanacs, edited by John Kettlewell. (Thomas Reed Publications, Boston, Massachusetts, 1992.)

A complete reference book for mariners. While not the sort of thing most people would read from cover to cover, it's great when you're looking for information on a specific boating subject.

APPENDIX D

RECOMMENDED WEBSITES

www.libertysails.com

Our personal website covering all of *Liberty*'s travels since we started cruising in 2003. Includes photos and advice for those interested in the cruising life.

www.nws.noaa.gov

Provides the latest forecasts and weather maps for the Atlantic, Pacific, and Gulf of Mexico. Under "radio fax products" look for consolidated daily weather briefings such as the one for the Northwest Atlantic at http://www.nws.noaa.gov/om/marine/nwatlanticbrief.shtml

www.navcen.uscg.gov/mwv/navrules/rotr_online.htm

The complete text of the Rules of the Road on the official U.S. Coast Guard site.

www.ssca.org

The site of the Seven Seas Cruising Association—an outstanding organization of cruisers helping cruisers.

www.yachtworld.com

This is where we found our current boat. If you're shopping for a boat or just enjoy looking at them, this site lists thousands for sale worldwide, complete with photos and detailed descriptions. Do an advanced search and find exactly the type of vessel you're interested in.

www.sailnet.com

While this is a commercial site for marine products, its main attractions are the message boards and over 1500 informative and entertaining articles about boating.

www.onpassage.com

This comprehensive site focuses on blue-water cruising, but there are many items of interest to all boaters.

www.womenaboard.com

A great site by and for women boaters.

www.boatingsafety.com/wow

While the main site is about safety (and well worth a look), the Women on Water section is a fun and entertaining place where women boaters can share experiences and learn.

www.womensailing.org

The organization is "dedicated to enriching the lives of women and girls through education and access to the sport of sailing." They have been supporting educational programs and supporting women in sailing nationwide since 1990.

www.worsa.org

The Women's Ocean Racing Sailing Association (WORSA), is a regional organization centered around Newport Beach and Dana Point Harbors in Orange County, California. It encourages the participation of women in sailing.

www.scya.org

The Southern California Yachting Association (SCYA) has a very active women's sailing program. They sponsor the SCYA Women's Sailing Convention that offers a broad selection of informative seminars for those who want to learn more and become more involved in sailing.

www.wsasmb.org

The Women's Sailing Association of Santa Monica Bay (WSASMB) is a regional organization that promotes and supports women's sailing.

About the Author

Commander Suzanne Giesemann, USN (Ret.) served twenty years in the United States Navy in a variety of assignments around the world, including special assistant to the Chief of Naval Operations, commanding officer of Transient Personnel Unit Puget Sound, and aide-de-camp to the chairman of the Joint Chiefs of Staff.

Since retiring from the Navy in 2003, she and her husband, Ty, have been cruising aboard their Morgan 46 sloop, *Liberty*. Their travels have taken them twice along the eastern seaboard from Newfoundland to the Bahamas, and across the Atlantic Ocean to the Mediterranean.

A U.S. Coast Guard licensed captain, Suzanne has been enjoying boats since she was two weeks old. She has served as a judge for *Cruising World* magazine's Boat of the Year competition. When not traveling and writing, she presents motivational seminars and teaches sailing.